ving that the child is exhibiting all the key indicators of a phase.
n will also display indicators from other phases.

---

elling

rovide an almost perfect match
ers are chosen on the basis of
conventional letter patterns.
l and becoming more like
evidence of self-constructed rules
ules. Writers copy, recall and
ir current understandings. They
number of words.

Phase 4: Transitional Spelling
(from sounds to structures)

In this phase writers are moving away from heavy reliance on the phonetic strategy towards the use of visual and meaning-based strategies. They may still have difficulty recognising if a word 'looks right' but should be able to proof their known bank of words. Writing will show evidence of an increasing bank of learned words. To help writers at this point it is better not to emphasise phonics but to extend their repertoire of alternative strategies. This is a critical phase in the development of spelling. It often takes writers a long time to move through it. It is important that progress is carefully monitored so as much support and explicit teaching can be given as possible. If writers do not receive sufficient support they may not progress beyond this phase.

Phase 5: Independent Spelling

In this phase writers have become aware of the many patterns and rules that are characteristic of the English spelling system. When spelling a new word they use a multi-strategy approach. They have the ability to recognise when a word doesn't look right and to think of alternative spellings. Spellers in this phase will have accumulated a large bank of known words that they can automatically recall. Independent spellers continue to use personal constructions when spelling unfamiliar words in draft writing. Independent spellers realise the importance of proof reading.

---

of sound without regard
tterns
ll substantial sounds in a

s for certain sounds often

de towards self as a

- ◆ uses letters to represent all vowel and consonant sounds in a word, placing vowels in every syllable
- ◆ is beginning to use visual strategies, such as knowledge of common letter patterns and critical features of words

is willing to take risks and accepts responsibility

See all Indicators in the Independent Phase (page 94).

is aware of social obligations as a speller

---

phases

osed to a wide variety of printed
which (at their own pace) they
t spelling.

ual patterns and common

ical features of words (i.e.
cs)
uilding up of a systematic
asis on the way:
rent sounds depending on
rd
ed by more than one letter or

t meaning as a strategy
of word banks by
high frequency and
se
ategies

Major Teaching Emphases

Transitional spellers need to develop familiarity with many common patterns of spelling through reading, writing and specific spelling activities.

They also need opportunities to focus on groups of words rather than words in isolation. This enables them to make generalisations about word patterns and to formulate rules.

- ◆ continue to emphasise visual patterns encouraging writers to focus on patterns and to classify words
- ◆ focus on word meaning and word derivations as a guide to spelling, e.g. sign - signature
- ◆ teach strategies for remembering the correct spelling of difficult words
- ◆ teach strategies for spelling new words
- ◆ encourage writers to generate alternative spelling in order to select the right one
- ◆ encourage writers to hypothesise and generalise, e.g. rules for plurals and syllabification
- ◆ encourage the use of words not previously used to enlarge spelling vocabulary
- ◆ continue the development of Word Banks and class alphabetical lists
- ◆ continue to model and teach proof-reading skills

Major Teaching Emphases

Independent spellers should be encouraged to accept responsibility for extending their spelling vocabulary. They should proof read all their written work as they are now able to spell most commonly used words correctly.

- ◆ focus on meaning as a guide to spelling
- ◆ continue to explore derivations of words—meanings of foreign words as a guide to spelling
- ◆ consolidate and extend proof-reading skills
- ◆ continue to build up a systematic picture of the whole spelling system
- ◆ teach writers to use context as a guide to spelling
- ◆ reinforce strategies for remembering correct spelling of difficult words
- ◆ emphasise social importance of spelling—insist on correct spelling for public audiences, parents, other classes or principal

Phases

Phase 1: Preliminary Spelling

In this phase children become aware that print carries a message. They experiment with writing-like symbols as they try to represent written language. Their writing is not readable by others as understandings of sound-symbol relationships have yet to develop. Children are fascinated by print and are constantly trying to explore the relationships between written and spoken words and between letters and sounds through emulating adults in role play of reading and writing.

Phase 2: Semi-Phonetic Spelling

In this phase children show developing understanding of sound-symbol relationships. Their spelling attempts show some evidence of sound-symbol correspondence. They may represent a whole word with one, two or three letters. In this, as in all phases of development children will be copying, recalling and inventing words. Children at this phase are able to copy letter by letter.

Phase 3: Phonetic S

In this phase writers are able to
between letters and sounds. Let
sound often without regard for
Spelling attempts are meaningf
standard spelling. There is ofte
that may not conform to adult
construct words according to th
use rote recall for an increasing

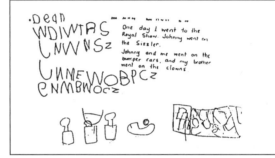

Key Indicators

- ◆ is aware that print carries a message
- ◆ uses writing-like symbols to represent written language
- ◆ uses known letters or approximations of letters to represent written language
- ◆ assigns a message to own symbols

is confident to experiment with words

- ◆ uses left to right and top to bottom orientation of print
- ◆ relies on the sounds which are most obvious to him or her
- ◆ represents a whole word with one, two or three letters. Uses mainly consonants

is confident to experiment with words— sees it as a problem-solving task

- ◆ chooses letters on the basis
for conventional spelling p
- ◆ sounds out and represents
word
- ◆ develops particular spelling
using self-formulated rules

*has a positive attitu
speller*

Major Teaching Emphases

Preliminary spellers need to be immersed in print. The environment should support the development of concepts of print and stimulate them to write.

- ◆ develop an awareness of letter names
- ◆ develop understandings of concepts of print
- ◆ use correct terminology for letters, sounds, words and sentences

At all phases:

- ◆ model writing in a variety of contexts
- ◆ encourage students to reflect on their spelling strategies
- ◆ encourage children to reflect on their understandings, gradually building a complete picture of the spelling system
- ◆ ensure that students have opportunities to write for a variety of audiences and purposes
- ◆ encourage students to take risks and have-a-go at spelling words they need to write

Major Teaching Emphases

Semi-Phonetic spellers need to be exposed to print in natural and meaningful contexts. They need opportunities to experiment with writing so they will develop understandings about print.

- ◆ help children develop a stable concept of a word
- ◆ help children to hear different sounds in words
- ◆ help children develop the ability to segment spoken words into individual sounds
- ◆ help children to represent sounds heard in words with letters written in the order they are heard
- ◆ select high interest and high frequency words from children's reading and class writing to add to class word lists
- ◆ teach children that letter names are constant but the sounds they represent vary
- ◆ provide many opportunities for children to explore and identify sound-symbol relationships in meaningful contexts

Major Teaching Em

Phonetic spellers should be ex
materials to provide data from
can draw new conclusions abo

- ◆ teach writers to look for vis
letter sequences in words
- ◆ teach writers to identify cr
differentiating characterist
- ◆ continue to emphasise the
view of spelling with emph
  - (a) letters can represent diff
context or place in the w
  - (b) a sound can be represent
letters
- ◆ teach writers to think abou
- ◆ continue the development
incorporating theme, topi
interesting words as they a
- ◆ introduce proof-reading st

Developmental Continuum

...erving that the child is exhibiting all the key indicators of a phase.
...dren will also display indicators from other phases.

...pelling

... provide an almost perfect match
...tters are chosen on the basis of
... conventional letter patterns.
...ul and becoming more like

... basis of sound without
...al spelling patterns e.g.
..., birgla (burglar),
...l (people), sum (some),

...ents all substantial
... ktn (kitten), wacht
...other), aftrwoods
...yclone), spidr (spider),
...st (next), peepl (people)

...ellings for certain
...lf-formulated rules, e.g.
...vas), wher (were)/whas
...saw)/mor (more), hape
...oot (put)/wood

... for those with similar
...cean), nacher (nature), wold
...ays (disobeys), consert
..., tuched (touched), daw
...ort (thought)

...er a correct vowel or
...derum (drum), miu (my), fiene
...(before), seing (sing)

...ferent ways according to the
...opped), watcht (watched),

...nt a syllable, e.g. watr

...ds, e.g. pell (pill), yellow
...t (let), sow (saw)

... of a two letter blend or
...k (milk), leve (leave), plak

...strategies e.g. awa (away),
...ht), lrst (last), cav (cave)

...bining known sight words
...eight (appreciate),
...hursday (Mother's Day)

...ed sight words correctly, e.g.
...re

...in words, e.g. ...ing, th...,

...cation for spelling longer
...one), butufl (beautiful). Some

...dge of similar sounding words

...vords in different ways

...as been gained from reading
...books, e.g. pirate, ship

...homonyms and homophones
...ark, their/there, one/won,

...pelling

...er and speller.

Phase 4: Transitional Spelling
(from sounds to structures)

In this phase writers are moving away from heavy reliance on the phonetic strategy towards the use of visual and meaning-based strategies. They may still have difficulty recognising if a word 'looks right', but should be able to proof their known bank of words. Writing will show evidence of an increasing bank of learned words.

- ◆ **uses letters to represent all vowel and consonant sounds in a word, placing vowels in every syllable, e.g. holaday (holiday), gramous (grandma's), castel (castle), replyd (replied), gorrillas (gorillas)**
- ◆ **is beginning to use visual strategies, such as knowledge of common letter patterns and critical features of words, e.g. silent letters, double letters**
- • uses visual knowledge of common English letter sequences when attempting to spell unknown words, e.g. thousend (thousand), cort (caught), doller (dollar)
- • uses vowel digraphs liberally, but may be unsure of correct usage, e.g. plaiyed (played), kaingarows (kangaroos), ailyen (alien)
- • may have over-generalised the use of silent 'e' as an alternative for spelling long vowel sounds, e.g. mite (might), biye (buy), chare (chair), moste (most), rane (rain), growe (grow), ocaye (okay)
- • syllabifies and correctly inserts a vowel before the 'r' at the end of a word, e.g. 'brother' instead of 'brothr', 'water' instead of 'watr'
- • spells inflectional endings such as ...tion, ...ious, ...ight, ...ious conventionally
- • includes all the correct letters but may sequence them incorrectly, e.g. yuo (you), shose (shoes), Micheal (Michael), thier (their), recieve (receive)
- • is beginning to make spelling generalisations, e.g. uses some double letters correctly
- • is able to proof read known bank of words
- • is beginning to use knowledge of word meanings, e.g. sign/signature, medicine/medical, circle/circular
- • usually represents all syllables when spelling a word, e.g.. uncontrollablely (uncontrollably)
- • is extending bank of known words that are used in writing, including some subject specific words, e.g. February, Christmas, restaurant, diameter, conservation, scientific
- • is beginning to use knowledge of word parts, e.g. prefixes, suffixes, compound words
- • uses more difficult homonyms and homophones correctly, e.g. sore/soar, pour/poor, board/bored
- • is willing to 'have a go' at spelling specialised words found in specific subject areas such as science and social studies, e.g. experament (experiment), abatories (abattoirs), lattitude (latitude), electrisity (electricity)
- • is aware of the importance of standard spelling for published work
- • is willing to use a range of resources
- • has an interest in words and enjoys using them

Phase 5: Independent Spelling

In this phase writers have become aware of the many patterns and rules that are characteristic of the English spelling system. When spelling a new word they use a multi-strategy approach. They have the ability to recognise when a word doesn't look right and to think of alternative spellings. Spellers in this phase will have accumulated a large bank of known words that they can automatically recall.

- ◆ **is aware of the many patterns and rules that are characteristic of the English spelling system, e.g. common English letter patterns, relationship between meaning and spelling**
- ◆ **makes generalisations and is able to apply them to new situations, e.g. rules for adding suffixes, selection of appropriate letter patterns (-ion)**
- ◆ **accurately spells prefixes, suffixes, contractions, compound words**
- ◆ **uses context to distinguish homonyms and homophones**
- ◆ **uses silent letters and double consonants correctly**
- ◆ **effectively spells words with uncommon spelling patterns and words with irregular spelling, e.g. aisle, quay, liaise**
- ◆ **uses less common letter patterns correctly, e.g. weird, forfeit, cough, reign**
- ◆ **uses a multi-strategy approach to spelling (visual patterns, sound patterns, meaning)**
- ◆ **is able to recognise if a word doesn't look right and to think of alternative spellings**
- ◆ **analyses and checks work, editing writing and correcting spelling**
- ◆ **recognises word origins and uses this information to make meaningful associations between words**
- ◆ **continues to experiment when writing new words**
- ◆ **uses spelling references such as dictionaries, thesauruses and resource books appropriately**
- ◆ **uses syllabification when spelling new words**
- ◆ **has accumulated a large bank of known sight words and is using more sophisticated language**
- ◆ **shows increased interest in the similarities, differences, relationships and origins of words**
- ◆ **is willing to take risks and responsibilities and is aware of a writer's obligations to readers in the area of spelling**
- ◆ **has a positive attitude towards self as a speller**
- ◆ **has an interest in words and enjoys using them**
- ◆ **is willing to use a range of resources and extend knowledge of words, including derivation, evolution and application**

© Education Department of Western Australia. Published by Longman Australia 1994. This page may be photocopied for classroom use only.

Year: _____ **Teacher:** _____

Year: _____ **Teacher:** _____

Year: _____ **Teacher:** _____

Year: _____ **Teacher:** _____

Indicators For Spelling I

Teachers can identify a child's phase of development by ob:
It should be noted however, that most chil

Phases

Phase 1: Preliminary Spelling

In this phase children become aware that print carries a message. They experiment with writing-like symbols as they try to represent written language. Their writing is not readable by others as understandings of sound-symbol relationships have yet to develop

- ◆ **is aware that print carries a message**
- ◆ **uses writing-like symbols to represent written language**
- ◆ **uses known letters or approximations of letters to represent written language**
- ◆ **assigns a message to own symbols**
- • knows that writing and drawing are different
- • knows that a word can be written down
- • draws symbols that resemble letters using straight, curved and intersecting lines
- • uses a combination of pictorial and letter representations
- • places letters randomly on a page
- • repeats some known alphabet symbols and often uses letters from own name
- • writes random strings of letters
- • shows beginning awareness of directionality
- • recognises own name or part of it, e.g. Stephen says 'That's my name' looking at 'Stop'
- • writes the first one or two letters of own name or word correctly and may finish with a random string of letters
- • writes own name correctly
- • names or labels own 'writing' and pictures using a variety of symbols
- • reacts to environmental print
- • is willing to have-a-go at writing
- • enjoys experimenting with writing-like forms
- • talks about what has been 'written' or drawn
- • asks questions about printed words, signs and messages
- • is keen to share written language discoveries with others

Phase 2: Semi-Phonetic Spelling

In this phase children show developing understanding of sound-symbol relationships. Their spelling attempts show some evidence of sound-symbol correspondence. They may represent a whole word with one, two or three letters.

- ◆ **uses left to right and top to bottom orientation of print**
- ◆ **relies on the sounds which are most obvious to him or her. This may be the initial sound, initial and final sounds, or initial, medial and final sounds, e.g. D (down),DN (down), DON (down), KT (kitten), WT (went), BAB (baby), LRFT (elephant)**
- ◆ **represents a whole word with one, two or three letters. Uses mainly consonants, e.g. KGR (kangaroo), BT (bit)**
- • uses an initial letter to represent most words in a sentence, e.g. s o i s g to c a s (Someone is going to climb a slide)
- • uses letter names to represent sounds, syllables or words, e.g. AT (eighty)
- • uses a combination of consonants with a vowel related to a letter name, e.g. GAM (game), MI (my)
- • writes one or two letters for sounds, then adds random letters to complete the word, e.g. greim (grass), rdms (radio)
- • begins to use some simple common letter patterns e.g. th (the), bck (bike)
- • uses a small bank of known sight words correctly
- • recognises some sound-symbol relationships in context, e.g. points to 'ship' and says 'sh' or recognises first letter of name
- • knows the letters of the alphabet by name
- • recognises some words in context, e.g. 'That says 'dog''
- • recognises rhyming words
- • recognises and copies words in the environment
- • leaves spaces between word-like letter clusters, e.g. I h bn sik (I have been sick)
- • confuses words with objects they represent, e.g. 'Train is a long word, 'cos trains are long. Butterfly is a little word...'
- • is willing to have a go at representing speech in print form
- • is confident to experiment with words
- • talks about what has been drawn, written
- • seeks response by questioning
- • is keen to share written language discoveries with others

Phase 3: Phonetic S

In this phase writers are able to between letters and sounds. Le sound often without regard fo Spelling attempts are meaning standard spelling.

- ◆ **chooses letters on the regard for convention kaj (cage), tabl (table, vampia (vampire), pe bak (back)**
- ◆ **sounds out and repres sounds in a word, e.g (watched), anathe (an (afterwards), siclon (c isgrem (icecream), ne**
- ◆ **develops particular sp sounds often using se becoz (because)/woz ((was), dor (door)/sor ((happy)/fune (funny), (would)**
- • substitutes incorrect letters pronunciation,e.g. oshan ((world), heard (herd), diso (concert), butiful (beautifu (door), tresher (treasure), t
- • adds an incorrect vowel af consonant, e.g. hait (hat), (fine), saeid (said), beofore
- • represents past tense in di sounds heard, e.g. stopt (s livd (lived)
- • uses the letter 'r' to repres (water), mothr (mother)
- • confuses short vowel soun (yellow), u (a), pan (pen), l
- • sometimes omits one lette digraph, e.g. fog (frog), m (plank)
- • still uses some letter name exellnt (excellent), mit (mig
- • creates some words by cor and patterns e.g. apreeshe jenyouwine (genuine), Ma1
- • usually spells commonly us in, has, his, he, my, the, he
- • uses some known patterns sh..., nght (night)
- • is beginning to use syllabif words, e.g. telefon (teleph syllables may be omitted
- • identifies and uses knowle
- • experiments with spelling
- • applies knowledge which and words encountered in
- • is beginning to use simple correctly, e.g. wind, read, for/four, too/to
- • is willing to have-a-go at s
- • sees self positively as a wri

Year: _____ **Teacher:** _____

Year: _____ **Teacher:** _____

Year: _____ **Teacher:** _____

Year: _____ **Teacher:** _____

SPELLING

DEVELOPMENTAL

CONTINUUM

The Spelling Developmental Continuum was researched, developed and written by Diana Rees, Education Department of Western Australia, in collaboration with Judith Rivalland, Edith Cowan University.

First Steps was developed by the Education Department of Western Australia under the direction of Alison Dewsbury.

Addison Wesley Longman Australia Pty Limited
95 Coventry Street
Melbourne 3205 Australia

Offices in Sydney, Brisbane and Perth, and associated
companies throughout the world.

Published by Addison Wesley Longman Australia on behalf of the
Education Department of Western Australia.

Designed by Kikitsa Michalantos
Produced by Addison Wesley Longman Australia Pty Ltd
Printed in Malaysia through Longman Malaysia, TCP

National Library of Australia
Cataloguing-in-Publication data

Spelling: developmental continuum.

ISBN 0 582 91569 4.

1. English language - Orthography and spelling - Study
and teaching (Primary). 2. Language arts (Primary). I.
Western Australia. Education Dept. (Series: First steps
(Perth, W.A.)).

372.632044.

The
publisher's
policy is to use
**paper manufactured
from sustainable forests**

Contents

Part I: Foundations of First Steps   1

Linking Assessment to Teaching   2
Effective Learning: 'Pewit'   6
Effective Learning: 'The Three Rs'   10

Part II: About Spelling   13

Effective Communication Diagram   14
What Do We Know About Spelling?   15
How to Use the Spelling Developmental
   Continuum   16
Creating Effective Classroom Contexts   18

Part III: Phases of Spelling Development   21

Phase 1: Preliminary Spelling   22

Preliminary Spelling Indicators   23
Teaching Notes   24
Creating Effective Classroom
   Contexts   25
   Context 1: Modelled and Shared
    Reading   28
   Context 2: Complementary Activities   30
   Context 3: Independent Writing   31
   Context 4: Modelled and Shared
    Writing   33
   Context 5: Independent Reading   34
   Context 6: Sharing and Reflecting   35
   Preliminary Spelling Chart   36
   For Parents   37

Phase 2: Semi-Phonetic Spelling   38

Semi-Phonetic Spelling Indicators   39
Teaching Notes   40
Creating Effective Classroom
   Contexts   42
Context 1: Modelled and Shared
   Reading   45
Context 2: Complementary Activities   47
Context 3: Independent Writing   48
Context 4: Modelled and Shared
   Writing   49

Context 5: Independent Reading   50
Context 6: Sharing and Reflecting   51
Semi-Phonetic Spelling Chart   52
For Parents   53

Phase 3: Phonetic Spelling   54

Phonetic Spelling Indicators   55
Teaching Notes   56
Creating Effective Classroom
   Contexts   58
Context 1: Modelled and Shared
   Reading   61
Context 2: Complementary Activities   63
Context 3: Modelled and Shared
   Writing   65
Context 4: Independent Reading   67
Context 5: Independent Writing   68
Context 6: Sharing and Reflecting   70
Phonetic Spelling Chart   71
For Parents   72

Phase 4: Transitional Spelling   73

Transitional Spelling Indicators   74
Teaching Notes   75
Creating Effective Classroom
   Contexts   77
Context 1: Modelled and Shared
   Reading   80
Context 2: Complementary Activities   82
Context 3: Independent Reading   85
Context 4: Modelled and Shared
   Writing   86
Context 5: Independent Writing   88
Context 6: Sharing and Reflecting   90
Transitional Spelling Chart   91
For Parents   92

Phase 5: Independent Spelling   93

Independent Spelling Indicators   94
Teaching Notes   95
Creating Effective Classroom
   Contexts   96

Context 1: Modelled and Shared
   Reading   98
Context 2: Independent Reading   99
Context 3: Complementary Activities 100
Context 4: Independent Writing   103
Context 5: Modelled and Shared
   Writing   104
Context 6: Sharing and Reflecting   105
Independent Spelling Chart   106
For Parents   107

Part IV Profiles of Spelling Development   109

Student's Profile Sheets   110
Whole Class Profile Sheets   116
Whole Class Profile Sheets Key Indicators Only   123

Acknowledgements   126
Bibliography   128

Part I

Foundations of First Steps

In this section the philosophical and theoretical framework of First Steps is set out. Specific points are made about the teaching of children for whom English is a second language and some suggestions are made about factors which foster effective learning in the classroom.

Foundations of First Steps includes:

- Linking Assessment to Teaching
    The Developmental Continua
    Teaching Strategies
    Underlying Theoretical Assumptions
    Important Considerations
    Teaching Children for whom English is a Second Language

- Effective Learning
    Problem Solving
    Embeddedness
    Working Memory
    Interaction
    Time

- 'The Three Rs'
    Reflecting
    Representing
    Reporting

Linking Assessment to Teaching

In an increasingly complex world, re-evaluating methods of teaching and learning is important. At the same time, methods of evaluating development, especially in relation to testing, have become highly problematic. Effective teachers have always used systematic observation and recording as a means of assessment. The First Steps materials have been developed to give teachers an explicit way of mapping children's progress through observation. The Developmental Continua validate what teachers know about children.

The Developmental Continua

The continua have been developed to provide teachers with a way of looking at what children can actually do and how they can do it, in order to inform planning for further development. It is recognised that language learning is holistic and develops in relation to the context in which it is used. However, given the complexity of each mode of language, a continuum has been provided for reading, writing, spelling and oral language, in order to provide teachers with in-depth information in each one of these areas.

The Continua make explicit some of the indicators, or descriptors of behaviour, that will help teachers identify how children are constructing and communicating meaning through language. The indicators were extracted from research into the development of literacy in English-speaking children. It was found that indicators tend to cluster together, i.e. if children exhibit one behaviour they tend to exhibit several other related behaviours. Each cluster of indicators was arbitrarily called a 'phase'. This clustering of indicators into phases allows teachers to map overall progress while demonstrating that children's

language does not develop in a linear sequence. The concept of a phase was shown to be valid by the Australian Council for Educational Research in their initial research into the validity of the *Writing: Developmental Continuum*.

Individual children may exhibit a range of indicators from various phases at any one time. 'Key' indicators are used to place children within a specific phase, so that links can be made to appropriate learning experiences. Key indicators describe behaviours that are typical of a phase. Developmental records show that children seldom progress in a neat and well-sequenced manner; instead they may remain in one phase for some length of time and move rapidly through other phases. Each child is a unique individual with different life experiences so that no two developmental pathways are the same.

The indicators are not designed to provide evaluative criteria through which every child is expected to progress in sequential order. They reflect a developmental view of teaching and learning and are clearly related to the contexts in which development is taking place. That is, language development is not seen as a 'naturalistic' or universal phenomena through which all children progress in the same way. Children's achievements, however, provide evidence of an overall pattern of development which accommodates a wide range of individual difference.

Teaching Strategies

The other major purpose of these documents is to link phases of development to teaching strategies, in order to help teachers make decisions about appropriate practice in the light of children's development. It is important that within this framework teachers value individual difference and cultural diversity. **It is not intended that these** strategies are prescriptive; they offer a range of practices from which teachers might select, depending upon the purposes of any particular language program and the needs of the children in their class. The purpose of the Continua is to link assessment with teaching and learning in a way that will support children and provide practical assistance for teachers.

Underlying Theoretical Assumptions

The First Steps indicators and suggested activities have been based on the following theoretical assumptions:

- Language learning takes place through interactions in meaningful events, rather than through isolated language activities
- Language learning is seen as holistic; that is, each mode of language supports and enhances overall language development
- Language develops in relation to the context in which it is used; that is, it develops according to the situation, the topic under discussion, and the relationship between the participants
- Language develops through the active engagement of the learners
- Language develops through interaction and the joint construction of meaning in a range of contexts
- Language learning can be enhanced by learners monitoring their own progress
- The way in which children begin to make sense of the world is constructed through the language they use and reflects cultural understandings and values

It is important that the indicators and activities are interpreted from the perspective of these underlying assumptions about language learning.

Important Considerations

The First Steps materials have been designed to help teachers map children's progress and suggest strategies for further development. When making decisions about what to do next, there are a number of issues that need to be considered.

Teachers' actions, strategies and ways of interacting with children reflect particular values and assumptions about learning. Through these interactions, children construct a view of what 'counts' as literacy in a particular classroom setting. This is manifested in the way:

a) teachers make decisions about selecting materials and texts
b) activities are carried out using the materials and texts
c) teachers talk with children
d) children talk with each other
e) what gets talked about (topic)

The decisions made by teachers play a role in how children come to understand what counts as literacy. In some cases there may be major conflicting and competing value systems at work leading to a variety of outcomes.

For example, the text Cinderella implicitly constructs a particular view of the world which presents women in a stereotypical role, not necessarily reflecting the role of women in modern society.

Clearly the text can be used in a number of different ways. It might be used as a shared book experience in which the teacher engages the children in a reading of the text, developing talk around the concepts of print and the repeated patterns of the text. In focusing on these aspects, the teacher would be constructing a view of reading which places emphasis on print rather than the message and leaves the role of women, as presented in the text, unchallenged. However, if the teacher encouraged the children to talk about the text in a way that challenged this view, through talking about their own experience of women and presenting other literature, the teacher would begin the process of helping children to detect the values within text.

Moving from this activity to asking the children to draw a picture of their own siblings and write a description about them, the teacher's response will signal to children what is important. Focusing on spelling and grammar will indicate that correctness is valued above content, whereas focusing on the content by discussing the characteristics of their siblings and comparing these with the ugly sisters, enables the children to become 'critical' readers.

The teaching strategies that are used and the texts selected are very powerful transmitters of cultural knowledge and how children construct the task of learning to be literate. In relation to the texts selected, what seems to be critical is the way in which they are used, rather than merely trying to select the 'right' text, because all texts convey values of some sort.

Given that literacy learning is such a complex task, teachers will use a range of different strategies for different purposes according to the needs of the children. However, what seems to be important is that teachers are consciously aware of which strategies they are selecting, why, and how these actions will impact on the children's understanding of what counts as literacy.

Another aspect of decision making is related to recognition of the specific skills, attitudes and knowledge children bring to the classroom. In order to enable children to feel confident in their own abilities, it is important to recognise, value, consolidate and extend the diversity of children's competence through classroom practice.

When planning a language program which will put the suggested strategies from First Steps into practice, based on the knowledge gained through mapping the children's progress through the indicators, it may be useful to consider the following:

– What new ways of using and understanding language do you want children to develop?
– What sort of contexts will enable this development to occur?
– What sort of texts (oral, written, media, dramatic) will facilitate this learning?
– How will children need to be supported in processing these texts?

– What new skills, processing and knowledge might the children need explicit understanding of in order to complete the language task?
– What underlying values and assumptions encompass your literacy program?
– How will the interactions between you and the children facilitate your aims for literacy development?
– How can you help children to monitor their own progress?

Caroline Barratt-Pugh
Judith Rivalland

Teaching Children for whom English is a Second Language

(or children whose language of home differs from that of the teacher)

When teaching children for whom English is a second language it is important to recognise:

* the diversity and richness of experience and expertise that children bring to school
* cultural values and practices that may be different from those of the teacher
* that children need to have the freedom to use their own languages and to code-switch when necessary
* that the context and purpose of each activity needs to make sense to the learner
* that learning needs to be supported through talk and collaborative peer interaction
* that the child may need a range of 'scaffolds' to support learning and that the degree of support needed will vary over time, context and degree of content complexity
* that children will need time and support so that they do not feel pressured

- that supportive attitudes of peers may need to be actively fostered
- that it may be difficult to assess children's real achievements and that the active involvement of parents will make a great deal of difference, as will on-going monitoring.

Action Research in a wide range of classrooms over a four-year period indicates that effective teaching strategies for children for whom English is a second language and children whose language of home differs from that of the teacher are:

- Modelling
- Sharing
- Joint Construction of Meaning
- The provision of Scaffolds or Frameworks
- Involvement of children in self-monitoring of their achievements
- Open Questions

  Open Questions that are part of sharing or joint construction of meaning, e.g. questions such as 'Do you think we should do … or … to make it work?' or 'It was very clever to do that. How did you think of it?', are very helpful. When children are asked closed questions to which teachers already know the answers, such as 'What colour/shape/size is it?', children often feel threatened and tend to withdraw.

These factors are expanded in the 'Supporting Diversity' chapters in First Steps *Reading: Resource Book* and *Oral Language: Resource Book*.

Caroline Barratt-Pugh
Anna Sinclair

Effective Learning: PEWIT

Many factors enhance or inhibit learning. The following factors help children and adults learn effectively. They are reflected in the First Steps Developmental Continua and Resource Books and underpin all the teaching and learning activities.

- Problem-solving
- Embeddedness
- Working memory
- Interaction
- Time

Problem Solving

Effective learning occurs when children and adults are able to modify and extend their understandings in order to make sense of a situation which has challenged them. This is the essence of problem solving. Effective problem solvers are those who can:

- identify a specific concept or skill as one that is posing a problem
- decide to do something about it
- have a go at finding a solution, using a range of strategies
- keep going until they are satisfied that their new understandings or skills provide the solution they have been reaching for.

Children

Children are natural learners. Young children are constantly learning about their environment through interaction, exploration, trial and error and through 'having a go' at things. As a child's world of experience expands, so deeper understandings are constructed. Additional learning is always built upon existing foundations, and existing structures are constantly being adapted to accommodate fresh insights. Children use language to make sense of their world, imposing order on it and endeavouring to control it.

In coming to terms with the spoken and written language:

(i) children need to see clearly the purposes for talking and listening, reading and writing so that they can adopt goals for themselves

(ii) children are engaged in problem solving when they explore oral and written language in their environment, in play and in role-play

(iii) children are problem solving when they attempt to represent the written language on paper

(iv) children are problem solving when they attempt to represent oral language in print

Teachers

Teachers are faced with a multitude of challenges every day. How can a difficult concept be introduced? How can the classroom be constantly stimulating for children without risking teacher burn-out? How can a different management strategy be implemented without risk of losing control? How can new insights into gender equity be incorporated into the curriculum?

In implementing change, it is helpful if each challenge can be represented as a problem which can be solved using the technique of 'having a go'; trying out a strategy; reflecting on the result; and then having another go, having slightly modified the strategy, Teachers sometimes expect too much of themselves. They should not expect things to work perfectly first time round. The essence of problem-solving is that strategies and understandings are gradually refined over time. There is seldom one right or easy answer, but a whole range of solutions on a variety of levels that fit the children's needs, teachers' own personal styles and the demands of the tasks.

Embeddedness (Contextualisation)

Most people have had the experience of listening to a speaker and being totally unable to make sense of what is being said. In such circumstances one is apt to say 'I switched off. It didn't make a word of sense.' People need to be able to make connections between their own current understandings and new learning that is being undertaken. A person who knows nothing of mechanics may be quite unable to follow a lecture on car maintenance, but may be able to work things out if the car is there with the bonnet up and the parts clearly visible.

If the context and the problem are embedded in reality and make sense to the learner, then the learner can engage in productive problem solving. If the problem is not embedded in, and seen to be arising from, past experience, then rote learning may occur, but real learning, which is capable of generalisation, will probably not take place.

Children

Children learn effectively in contexts that make sense to them. The challenges which children face and the problems which they attack in their early environment are embedded in familiar, real life contexts. This can be seen quite clearly in early oral language development, when language acquisition is closely tied to the immediate environment and to current needs.

In coming to terms with written language:

(i)   children need to be given opportunities to interact with print (read and write) in contexts which make sense to them and which have their counterpart in the real world, in role play and in real situations, e.g. making shopping lists, identifying stop signs

(ii)   children need to see adults explicitly modelling reading and writing for a variety of purposes in real situations, e.g. reading and writing notes

(iii)   children need to interact not only with books, but with the wide range of print found in daily life, e.g. in newspapers and environmental print.

Teachers

Teachers also need to start from where they are, working within their own familiar context. The First Steps resources offer a number of alternative ways of looking at teaching and a great many strategies and activities which people have found to be useful. Once teachers have decided what problem they want to solve or what challenge they wish to take on, they need to start from a context which makes sense to them and gradually incorporate alternative strategies within their own repertoires. The new learning needs to be embedded within the context of the old and teaching strategies need to be slowly adapted to meet new challenges and different understandings.

Working Memory (Mental Space)

Working memory, which is sometimes called M-space, is very different from long or short term memory. It is, in effect, a measure of the number of discrete elements which the mind can cope with at any one time. A good analogy is that of the juggler, who can juggle competently with four or five balls, but when given one too many, will drop the lot.

Once ideas and skills become familiar as a result of practice over a period of time, two things happen. One is that the learner does not have to think consciously about how to do them any more, so much less space is taken up in the working memory, e.g. spelling a very familiar word. The other is that several different skills gradually become one skill. For example when learning to print children have to manipulate the pencil, remember the formation of letters and consider the order in which the marks have to appear on the page. With practice these individual skills will integrate to become one skill.

Any emotional issue or concern will 'fill up' the mental space more quickly than anything else. Fear, anger or worry may totally inhibit a person's capacity to learn. Most people have had the experience of being unable to concentrate because their mind is fully taken up by an all-consuming emotion. The only thing to do is to give oneself time to 'get it together' again. In the meantime performance on any task will be poor and will continue to deteriorate until the cloud of emotion has lifted. If people say 'I just couldn't think straight', they are usually speaking the truth.

Children

Children focus their entire attention on one element which they perceive to be a challenge. Young children can only cope with one or two different factors at once. As they get older they can juggle with an increasing number of elements, although there is a limit to the amount that anyone can handle.

In coming to terms with the written language:

(i) children may only be able to focus on one or two different factors at any one time. For example, during a shared reading lesson one child may focus on the meaning and spelling of an unusual word in a story, whereas another may be emotionally involved with the characters. Neither may have 'heard' the teacher explaining the use of speech marks.

(ii) as they focus on one skill children may temporarily lose competence in another very familiar skill. For example when a child is absorbed in getting ideas onto paper the quality of handwriting may deteriorate.

(iii) children need to practise and apply a particular aspect of language in a number of contexts until it becomes automatic. Opportunities to practise in stimulating circumstances constitute an important component of all language programs, so that 'mental space' is made available for more complex learning.

(iv) children may appear to make significant regressions if their 'mental space' is fully taken up with an emotional issue relating to home or school.

Teachers

Teachers sometimes make impossible demands on themselves. They are also only able to cope with a certain number of new things at any one time. Instead of attempting everything at once, they need to try one small component of a task first and then build on that. For instance, it is impossible to attempt to observe all the children in a class at once. The secret is to focus on only three or four children a week, looking only at the key indicators. Children thought to be at risk can gradually be placed on the continuum, looking at all indicators.

It is important not to try to do too much at once. If circumstances become overwhelming for any reason, such as trouble at home, too many extraneous duties or ill health, teachers should wait for things to calm down before trying anything new.

Interaction

Interaction is of fundamental importance to human beings. People need to discuss ideas, build on each other's expertise, use each other as sounding boards and work creatively as communities of learners. It is through talk that ideas are generated, refined and extended.

Children

Children need unlimited opportunities to interact with adults and with other children in their daily lives. They need to interact with others to plan, explore, problem-solve, question, discuss and direct their activities. In doing so they try out and modify their ideas. As they use language in social situations they refine their language use and learn more about how language works.

In coming to terms with the written language:

(i) children need freedom to interact with adults in discussions about writing and reading. These discussions should not always be dominated by adults. Children need opportunities to direct conversation. The adult role may be to provide feedback and reinforcement.

(ii) children need freedom to interact with their peers to discuss problems and to formulate and clarify their ideas as they write

(iii) children need to feel safe to ask for help when they need it.

(iv) children need freedom to experiment with written language in socially supportive situations.

Teachers

Teachers also need time and opportunities to interact with their colleagues. Often the most profitable interactions take place informally between staff members who trust and respect each other. Time can also be put aside at a regular meeting for a school staff to discuss and share professional issues and insights regarding the implementation of First Steps or interesting new initiatives being undertaken by different teachers. One school developed a sharing strategy whereby every staff member concentrated on one specific strategy for a week or two, after which all reported back. This school took advantage of the wealth of expertise which is to be found in any staff room.

It is also extremely helpful to interact with parents informally as well as in more formal conferences to share insights about the children. Interacting with children is also of crucial importance, encouraging a two-way process which will enrich both teacher and child as each listens and responds to the other. Conferences between teacher, parent and child as co-members of the community of learners can also be very profitable.

Time

Children

In their everyday lives children have time to construct understandings gradually through inquiry, exploration and problem solving. They also have time to consolidate and integrate these understandings through practice. The amount of time needed to practise new skills and learnings will vary from child to child. Some may need to apply these understandings in only a few situations before they come to terms with them. Others will need to apply the understandings more frequently and in a wider variety of situations before they can begin to generalise and transfer them.

In coming to terms with the written language:

(i) children need opportunities to have regular and on-going involvement in strategies such as shared book experiences, language experience and playing with language, in order to foster their understandings about how the written language works

(ii) children need opportunities to have regular involvement in activities which give them independent practice in their own time, at their own pace, as often as is needed in both reading and writing

Teachers

Teachers need to be as kind to themselves as they are to their children. They need to give themselves time for reflection; time for experimentation and having a go; time to refine and develop strategies already in place; time for sharing with colleagues and parents and time to enjoy their job. Every adult is growing and developing throughout life. Real growth takes time in every sphere of life and development can be enhanced but not hurried. Teachers need to be confident that they are comfortable with the strategies they are implementing and time will be on their side.

Effective Learning: 'The Three Rs'

Adults and children are all learners moving along a continuum. Teachers and children come together as a community of learners. All can benefit from the three Rs:

- Reflecting
- Representing
- Reporting

Reflecting

Children

Children need time to reflect on an experience and on what they have learned from it. Too often they hustle from one learning activity to another, with no time, no space and no structure to help them stand back and think about what they have learned. If they are encouraged to pause and reflect on the insights they have gained and on things that have suddenly started to make sense to them, they will consciously take control of their learning in a new way. They will develop an awareness of specific understandings and the place of those understandings in the overall scheme of things. They will come to value and respect themselves as learners and will become aware of their own learning processes.

Teachers

Teachers need to take time to reflect on their teaching practice. They need to congratulate themselves on their many successes, to consider their goals and take stock of their current situation. Studies have shown, for instance, that almost all primary school teachers firmly believe in developmental learning, but this is not always reflected in their approach to teaching. Teachers may reflect on their teaching practice by asking themselves questions such as: Are my beliefs and theoretical understandings reflected in my current classroom practice? Are the needs of all children being met? Are children engaged in active learning? Are they interacting effectively with others?

It is always worth taking time to reflect on the reality of daily classroom experience, to analyse strengths and to pin-point the areas that may need extra attention. Management strategies, interaction with parents, collaborative work with other staff members and teacher's own professional development are all areas which can provide food for thought from time to time.

Representing

Children

Children may need to represent their learning in a very concrete form. This may be by drawing a picture, constructing a diagram or by writing down their thoughts. In some learning areas such as maths or science it may involve constructing a model.

Teachers

Teachers may need to clarify their reflections by listing one or two items that seem to be significant. Even if no action is taken immediately, an insight will have been captured and recorded for future use. If an idea is written down it is likely to become a reality.

Reporting

Children

Children need to clarify their understandings by talking about them. Children refine, consolidate and extend their learning by reporting on what they know to a peer, a small group or their teacher. This type of reporting occurs best in a natural context when a child is not under any stress and does not feel 'on show.'

Teachers

Teachers may wish to contribute to the process of school planning by reporting on what they consider to be essential goals, strategies and issues for their schools and their students. Every staff member has a crucial contribution to make which will enrich and extend the operations of the school community. Too often the richness and depth of a teacher's experience is confined to one classroom instead of being available for all members of the educational community. All teachers need the support of every other teacher if children are to gain the full benefit of growing up in a community of learners.

Part II

About Spelling

This section provides some general information about spelling in the First Steps program. The three major tools of effective communication are oral (or non-verbal), language, writing and reading. Spelling is a sub-set of writing and can only be considered within the context of writing. It has been given special emphasis because society often uses spelling to make judgements about levels of literacy. 'About Spelling' includes:

- **Effective Communication**

- **What Do We Know About Spelling?**

- **How to Use the Spelling Developmental Continuum**
  Predict
  Collect Data
  Involve parents and children
  Link Assessment with Teaching
  Monitor Progress

- **Creating Effective Classroom Contexts**
  Modelled and shared reading
  Complementary activities
  Independent writing
  Modelled and shared writing
  Independent reading
  Sharing and reflecting
  Integrated and ongoing learning

My handsome dad is called Andrew. His work is selling guitars. He calls me Chloe. I like to go to his plays. He has brown hair. My dad gives me lots of presents. I don't like tickles. He loves to eat spagetti bolognaise. He is a bit of fat, a bit of thin. I love him because he loves me.

EFFECTIVE COMMUNICATION

EFFECTIVE COMMUNICATION can be achieved by focusing on activities based on purposeful language interactions. Purposeful talk is one of the major means through which children construct and refine their understandings of language. Talk should underpin all language activities.

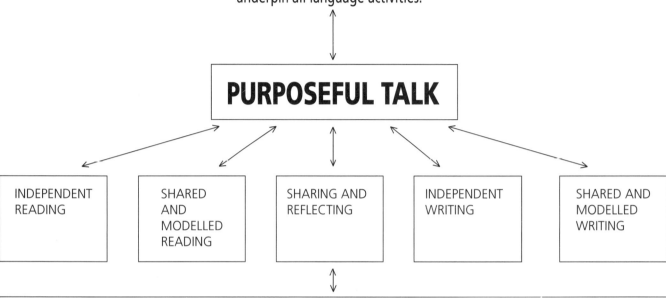

PURPOSEFUL TALK

| INDEPENDENT READING | SHARED AND MODELLED READING | SHARING AND REFLECTING | INDEPENDENT WRITING | SHARED AND MODELLED WRITING |

PURPOSEFUL TALK

Communication occurs when the speaker has effectively relayed his/her meaning to the listener.

Provide opportunities for:

- discussion across the curriculum;
- negotiation;
- group interaction;
- brainstorming;
- clarification of values and issues;
- reflective response to own and others' contributions;
- reading and retelling;
- storytelling;
- news telling;
- drama;
- reporting;
- debating and arguing;
- questioning and enquiring.

PURPOSEFUL WRITING

Communication occurs when the writer has effectively relayed his/her meaning to the reader.
Good spelling is a factor in effectively relaying meaning.

Provide opportunities for:

- learning about writing;
- learning through writing;
- analysing different forms in written context;
- modelled writing;
- editing;
- writing for different purposes and audiences; and
- self evaluation of writing development.

Encourage children to develop spelling skills through:

- word study activities, e.g. derivations, origins, morphemic units;
- visual patterning activities;
- identifying critical features of words;
- using spelling resources;
- word sorting;
- use of personal lists;
- proof reading;
- a range of strategies.

PURPOSEFUL READING

Effective communication occurs when a reader creates, interprets and analyses meanings from text.

Provide opportunities for:

- reading for a wide range of purposes;
- reading a wide variety of different text-types;
- critical reflection on and response to texts;
- discussion which encompasses different interpretations of and responses to text.

What Do We Know About Spelling?

1 The ability to spell easily and automatically enables us to become more effective writers. The less energy and thought we have to put into thinking about spelling, the more thought we can put into what is said.

2 Spelling is only one aspect of effective writing. Historically, however, levels of literacy have often been measured by spelling ability. Among employers in the 'public' arena this attitude still prevails. It is very important to be aware that generally someone is going to read what we write. We must take responsibility to see that spelling is correct. If we don't, people will make judgements about our level of literacy and sometimes even our intelligence.

3 Good spellers are self-monitoring and self-regulating. They take responsibility for getting spelling correct. They look for their own errors. They check words they are not sure of in a dictionary, or ask a friend. Ultimately all writers must take responsibility for ensuring their spelling is correct. Good spellers are not perfect spellers. They are people who can say, 'No that doesn't look right', and then check to see if the word is correct.

4 The English language is not a regular language, but it is systematic and patterned. Learning to spell is a process of working out the patterns and systems of the English language, then applying these understandings to new words as we encounter them. So, learning to spell entails learning to understand the systematic *code* by which English is written.

5 Learning to spell is not learning lists of words. It is a developmental process of learning to apply different strategies appropriately, so that we can spell correctly all the words we write. These strategies include sound sequences, knowledge of graphophonic relationships, visual patterns and meaning. In order to do this, we need to learn to classify, hypothesise, generalise, look for patterns and relationships, and seek to understand the relationships between meaning and spelling. **Spelling is a thinking process not a rote learning task.**

6 Understanding spelling helps writers to make better meaning when they write. Good spellers understand the links between word meaning and spelling. Investigating word meanings not only guides us to spell words correctly, but helps develop a diverse vocabulary. If our first-draft writing is reasonably legible and contains few spelling errors we can easily find the parts that need revision as we read.

Teacher's Role

It is the teacher's role to make these understandings explicit as he or she talks with children about spelling and writing. With this knowledge, children will see good reasons for making the effort to improve their spelling.

How to Use the Spelling Developmental Continuum

- **Predict** where the children are on the Continuum by looking at the Key Indicators
- **Collect Data** to confirm the prediction, through observation and collection of work samples
- **Involve** parents and children
- **Link Assessment with Teaching** by referring to the major teaching emphases
- **Monitor Progress** through on-going collection of data and consultation with parents and linking children's current phase of development with teaching

Predict

- Read through the Overview of the Spelling Developmental Continuum, with special reference to the Phase Descriptions and Key Indicators.
- Match your knowledge of the children in your class with the Phase Descriptions and Key Indicators to predict which phase each child is in. Experience shows that it takes about thirty seconds to place a child on the Continuum in this way.

Collect Data

The Continuum indicators will help you gather information about children's spelling behaviours. Your data collection will be gained through observation of children writing and their draft written products generated as they take part in regular writing activities, writing for a range of purposes and audiences.

Place Children on the Continuum

- Children who are exhibiting all the Key Indicators of a phase are operating in that phase. If they are not yet exhibiting all the Key Indicators of a phase they are operating in the phase before.
- For most of the children in a class it is only necessary to look at the Key Indicators.
- If you choose to look at more than the Key Indicators you will expect and find that children may display behaviours across two or three phases. It is the Key Indicators, however, that are used to determine which phase children are operating in. This information is designed to inform and guide the teaching program.
- For children who are at risk and are experiencing difficulties teachers may wish to look at *all* the indicators because:
  - the complete range of indicators comprises a sensitive and fine-grained diagnostic tool that enables teachers to focus on children's current understandings and the strategies they are using. The information obtained provides insights into children's thinking and an individualised guide to teaching;
  - it is sometimes difficult to measure the progress of children at risk, and it may appear that they are making little or no progress. It is encouraging for teachers, parents and the children themselves to be aware of the tiny but crucial gains that are actually being made;
  - it is sometimes tempting to talk about children at risk in terms of what they *cannot* do. A focus on the achievement of behavioural indicators leads to a celebration of what children *can* do and an accurate assessment of how much they are learning.
- If a class contains several children at risk, it is suggested that only one of these children is observed for at least two weeks before concentrating on the next child.

Involve Parents and Children

Parents often have a very clear sense of their children's competencies. They are usually pleased to be asked to comment on what they have observed at home. Including parents in the assessment and monitoring process by asking for their observations may help you to gain an extremely accurate picture of the children.

Once parents can see where their children are on the Continuum they will be interested in reading the pages of ideas that suggest how they may be able to further support their children's development at home.

Children are also keenly interested in their own progress and enjoy using the check list for children entitled *Things I Can Do*. Experience has shown that very often children are their own harshest critics.

Link Assessment With Teaching

When children are placed in phases, the section entitled Major Teaching Emphases will guide the selection of appropriate teaching strategies and activities. Many of these are described in some detail in this book. Others are discussed in the accompanying *First Steps Spelling: Resource Book*. The key teaching strategies described in each phase are considered to be critical for children's further development. They can be used to meet the needs of a whole class, small groups and individual children.

Monitor Progress

The Developmental Continuum provides a sensitive and accurate means by which progress can be monitored over time. This involves further observation and data collection. Links are constantly made between assessment and teaching.

The spelling record forms may be used to map individual or class progress. If entries are dated it is easy to see how a child is progressing. The record forms may also be used as a basis for reporting to parents.

Many schools synthesise class records twice a year to monitor overall progress and to inform the allocation of resources and support.

Creating Effective Classroom Contexts

Spelling arises from and informs reading and writing. It is through reading that children discover print and through reading and writing that they explore it. Reading reinforces children's understandings about the meaning of words and the relationships between them and so fosters their ability to use the semantic and syntactic cuing systems. It helps them develop and extend their knowledge of graphophonics and it exposes them to word models which they can use as referents. Spelling is a writer's tool. As they focus on spelling in the context of writing, children develop a systematic understanding of the way the graphophonic system works. This, in turn, provides children with decoding knowledge which they can use as they read. In itself spelling has no purpose and no audience, but in the context of writing, spelling becomes very important to both purpose and audience. It is important for children to realise that a 'public audience' will always make harsh judgements about poor spelling and that good spelling is a vital component of communication through writing.

Six contexts are used throughout this text as frameworks for presenting teaching strategies and activities and helping teachers monitor spelling behaviours. For convenience of access these strategies are labelled Context One, Context Two, etc., but it is stressed that the order in which they are presented is not significant. The contexts are listed and described below.

Context 1: Modelled and Shared Reading

Modelled and shared reading sessions enable children to interact with print in exciting and purposeful ways as they construct understandings about words, how they look and how they work together to create meaning. Modelling and sharing sessions provide excellent contexts for fostering awareness and refining understandings through talk.

Context 2: Complementary Activities

Complementary activities reinforce the learning which has taken place in shared reading and writing sessions. Children need to encounter and engage with a concept or strategy in a range of different contexts so that they can clarify their understandings and become more skilled in their use of a strategy through purposeful practice.

Context 3: Independent Writing

Independent writing opportunities engage children in writing for many different purposes and audiences, both in real life and in play. Children need to talk as they write. They will use these opportunities to experiment with and apply the understandings they have gained in the shared reading session.

Context 4: Modelled and Shared Writing

Modelled and shared writing sessions enable teachers to introduce children to spelling strategies and the use of words in a wide range of different forms of writing. These sessions show how successful writers meet challenges as the teacher 'thinks aloud'; solving problems and making decisions. The interactive nature of these sessions gives them special value. Teachers are able to reinforce and extend developing understandings, providing opportunities for heightening children's awareness and enabling them to generalise their understandings. Proof-reading and editing skills can be modelled effectively in this context.

Context 5: Independent Reading

Independent reading opportunities engage children in the creation of meaning, enabling them to come to grips with concepts and conventions of print and the representation of words in print. Children sometimes like to read peacefully by themselves, but they need to know they can ask questions and discuss issues with peers should the need arise.

Context 6: Sharing and Reflecting

Sharing and reflecting on ideas, processes and products is crucial to the learning process. Children need to be given time, opportunity and support as they think about what they have learned, talk about it with others and represent it in ways which make sense to them. It is through reflection and talk that explicit understandings about the spelling system can be clarified and focused.

Integrated and Ongoing Learning

In all these contexts children construct understandings about spelling and develop spelling strategies that enable them to be effective writers. It is because children meet the challenge of spelling every time they want to write that they realise how important it is to write words that other people can read.

For young writers the cognitive demands of spelling are great, so the sooner children are able to automate spelling, the more they will be able to focus on the content of their writing. It is important that this is discussed with children explicitly.

The order in which children participate in these learning contexts will be dictated by the teacher's objectives and the nature of the strategies and activities employed. The contexts are presented in the same order only to enable ease of access for teachers using this book.

Part III

Phases of Spelling Development

By scanning the phase descriptions and key indicators on the overview sheet at the beginning of this book, teachers can place children in a phase of the Spelling Continuum. Placement can be validated by examining samples of children's work. Part III of this book provides details of each phase, including all indicators and a wide range of appropriate teaching strategies.

Each phase includes:
- a sample of children's writing showing specific indicators
- indicators describing children's behaviour
  key indicators are marked ◆ and written in bold print

Teaching Notes
- a description of the major teaching emphases
- an example of a possible teaching sequence
- a range of appropriate strategies and activities under the following headings:
  – Shared or Modelled Reading
  – Complementary Activities
  – Independent Writing
  – Modelled and Shared Writing
  – Independent Reading
  – Sharing and Reflecting
- a page for parents

On the weekend my dad let me borrow his colourful hat and I hid under it.

Preliminary Spelling

In this phase children become aware that print carries a message. They experiment with writing-like symbols as they try to represent written language. Their writing is not readable by others as understandings of sound-symbol relationships have yet to develop.

In the holiday I was in the newspaper (teacher-written). The child's name is Sam. S, a and m can clearly be seen, mixed up with other letters and letter-like formations.

Children are fascinated by print and are constantly trying to explore the relationships between written and spoken words and between letters and sounds through emulating adults in role play of reading and writing.

The Writer:
◆ **is aware that print carries a message**
◆ **uses writing-like symbols to represent written language**
◆ **uses known letters or approximations of letters to represent written language**
◆ **assigns a message to own symbols**
• shows beginning awareness of directionality
• knows that writing and drawing are different
• knows that a word can be written down
• draws symbols that resemble letters
• is willing to have-a-go at representing speech in print form
• enjoys experimenting with writing-like forms
• talks about what has been 'written' or drawn

Preliminary Spelling Indicators

The Writer:

◆ **is aware that print carries a message**
◆ **uses writing-like symbols to represent written language**
◆ **uses known letters or approximations of letters to represent written language**
◆ **assigns a message to own symbols**
• knows that writing and drawing are different
• knows that a word can be written down
• draws symbols that resemble letters using straight, curved and intersecting lines
• uses a combination of pictorial and letter representations
• places letters randomly on a page
• repeats some known alphabet symbols and often uses letters from own name
• writes random strings of letters
• shows beginning awareness of directionality
• recognises own name or part of it, e.g. Stephen says 'That's my name' looking at 'Stop'
• writes the first one or two letters of own name or word correctly and may finish with a random string of letters
• writes own name correctly
• names or labels own 'writing' and pictures using a variety of symbols
• reacts to environmental print
• is willing to have-a-go at representing speech in print form
• enjoys experimenting with writing-like forms
• talks about what has been 'written' or drawn
• asks questions about printed words, signs and messages
• is keen to share written language discoveries with others.

Teaching Notes

At this level of spelling development, children begin to use symbols from the alphabet to represent words. Children's understanding of the link between the alphabet and the message is not yet clear but their interest in it shows they are aware of its importance in writing. Although other people are unable to read their 'writing' because children do not yet know how to link letters and sounds, they attempt to use letters and letter-like formulations as they know that these hold the key to communication.

Writing provides the context for spelling development. As children are given opportunities to 'write' frequently, they become aware that conventional print is different from the marks they are making. Their writing slowly begins to take on the characteristics of conventional print; this is the beginning of spelling development. In the pre-primary stage many opportunities to write are provided informally and the decision on whether or not to write remains with the child. After this all children need to take part in daily writing sessions. Behaviours exhibited in any one classroom may range from the preliminary to the transitional phases.

Major Teaching Emphases

Preliminary spellers need to be immersed in print. The environment should support the development of concepts of print and stimulate them to write.

- ◆ **develop an awareness of letter names**
- ◆ **develop understandings of concepts of print**
- ◆ **use correct terminology for letters, sounds, words and sentences**
- • develop awareness that writing is purposeful
- • develop awareness that written language communicates a message
- • establish an environment of constant and natural language use
- • encourage children to write and experiment with print
- • provide authentic contexts for conveying written messages

At all phases:
- ◆ **model writing in a variety of contexts**
- ◆ **encourage students to reflect on their spelling strategies**
- ◆ **encourage children to reflect on their understandings, gradually building a complete picture of the spelling system**
- ◆ **ensure that students have opportunities to write for a variety of audiences and purposes**
- ◆ **encourage students to take risks and have-a-go at spelling words they need to write.**

◆ *Entries in bold are considered critical to the children's further development.*

Creating Effective Classroom Contexts

If there are children in a Pre-Primary Unit who are Preliminary spellers, they will learn through interaction with people and print, play, role play and experimentation. It is not recommended that these children receive formal instruction. Their curiosity and eagerness to solve problems will support their learning as it has in the past and their needs will be met by the teacher as they arise across a range of contexts.

The following teaching sequence illustrates how a strategy or understanding, in this case the awareness of a letter and the sound it represents, can be introduced and threaded through the day in a year one class using the six major contexts previously described (shared and modelled reading, complementary activities, independent writing, shared and modelled writing, independent reading, sharing and reflecting sessions). Activities will be structured for individuals, small groups or the whole class, according to the children's needs and the demands of context, purpose and audience.

Modelled and Shared Reading

A first reading of any text is designed purely for pleasure. In subsequent readings of the text, the teacher may focus on a letter that features the initial letter of some children's names. Children can then scan the text and take turns to circle all the words that feature the targetted letter. Children can say the names and words to each other to see if they can identify a common sound. If some children do not seem to 'hear' the sound, do not worry. All the children will be able to visually identify the letter. It is important that the letter is called by its name, because letter names are constant whereas the sound they represent may not be.

Complementary Activities

Children can then undertake a 'word search', looking round the room to identify words featuring the targeted letter. All the words found by the children are written on a chart. Some children may still be using the visual image to identify the letter and may not yet connect the letter with the sound it represents.

It is vital that children take the initiative as they conduct their word search. As long as they are in control of the process they will understand what is going on. The search will continue over a long period of time as children add words to the lists.

At this stage the teacher will be able to observe which children have made the links between the letter and the sound it represents.

Independent Writing

Children can now participate in activities which stem from the text they have shared. They may like to draw and label their picture . Within the class some children's writing may consist of scribble, letter-like formations or letters from their name. Others may write the initial letters of words, the initial and final letters or maybe even some medial letters. Children will work as individuals, but there will be much interaction as they help each other and thus clarify their understandings. The teacher will observe which children have made the connection between an individual sound and symbol and are writing a letter with understanding.

Modelled Writing

In this session the teacher might choose to write a rhyme based loosely on the original text. Every time the teacher models the writing process, one aim will be to illustrate the sound-symbol relationship under consideration so that children are confident and equipped to apply the concept in their own writing. Children who have moved beyond the initial concept will explore more complex or different relationships.

Independent Reading

There will be many times during the day when children choose to look at books. They will also interact with print in the classroom such as charted songs and rhymes, children's 'news', weather reports or informational texts. During these times children will often notice the letters they have focused on and will consolidate their understanding of that sound-symbol relationship.

Sharing and Reflecting

Children need affirmation that they are productive and effective learners. They gain this affirmation as they see that others value what they have learned. Young children are often unable to stand back from the situation and think about what they have learned unless ways of doing this are modelled for them and opportunities structured for them to have-a-go at it. It is sometimes valuable to encourage children to role play being teachers so that they can teach a class of toys or a puppet what they themselves have learned.

The value of reflective talk is often considerably greater to the speaker than to the listener, as talking triggers reflection and helps to catch, clarify and consolidate the thoughts.

Use the class spelling chart (see page 36) as a focus for the sharing and reflection sessions. Encourage children to add words they have discovered under the appropriate child's name.

Integrated and On-going Learning

The pathway described above demonstrates how the shared reading session was used to foster children's awareness of a sound-symbol relationship. Children were given an opportunity to experiment with and apply the concept in their own writing. Complementary activities were undertaken to reinforce, extend and consolidate their understanding. Children who had developed a sound grasp of the concept were encouraged to undertake further exploration. A modelled writing session re-focused the children's attention so that they were prepared and equipped for independent reading activities. During the day every opportunity was taken to support children's learning of the chosen concept in contexts which made sense to them, through further modelled and independent writing, shared reading or complementary activities. Through open-ended activities, children who had already firmly established the learning outcome were able to further extend their understandings. At the end of the day children had a strong sense of what they had learned and achieved. As they were able to focus on, share and report on their learning, their image of themselves as learners was positively reinforced.

Teaching strategies for Phase 1: Preliminary Spelling are described in the following pages under the headings of the six major contexts.

Context 1: Modelled and Shared Reading

Reading with children is a wonderful way of extending the shared reading experiences children have had at home. It is in the context of shared and modelled reading that a great deal of productive teaching and learning takes place about the way that written language works, the processes readers use and the strategies writers employ.

The activities which the teacher employs are all designed to provide a context within which holistic and generalised understandings can develop. Within the context of modelled and shared reading, aspects of spelling can be effectively developed.

Teaching Suggestions

When choosing or creating texts of different types and print styles, include:
- a range of alphabet books.
- books of rhymes, poetry and songs, containing familiar words, phrases and rhymes that will help children further develop their concept of a word and understanding of graphophonic relationships.
- classroom print:
  - favourite songs, rhymes and recipes
  - wall stories, labels, simple instructions, weather report, etc.

Modelled and shared reading provide opportunities for teachers to support the development of children's understanding of literacy and language. Specific understandings related to spelling include:
  - the importance of taking risks
  - the understanding that a word can be written down
  - the concept of directionality
  - the concept of a word as a unit of print with space on either side
  - some strategies that readers use, including:
    semantic cues
    graphophonic cues.
- Create an environment which fosters questioning, inquiry, comment and criticism, encouraging children to read and comment on messages, notices and lists which are displayed in the classroom.
- Place a list of all the children's names at child level, so that they can find their own names and those of their friends.
- Talk about the different components of letters, birthday cards, recipes and lists etc. and how these arise from the different purposes of the texts. Children will begin to understand that the structure of the text helps them decode the words, e.g. 'love from Kim' on a letter or card.

- Introduce the children to 'Secret Messages' (see *Spelling: Resource Book* Chapter 3).
- Introduce the children to 'Word Sorting' using very familiar words and children's names, and sorting according to initial letters (see *Spelling: Resource Book*, Chapter 4).
- Share the reading and chanting of rhymes and tongue twisters that focus on particular sounds or rhyming words. Place these on charts where children can refer to them.
- Use pictures as a source of discussion about rhyming words, e.g. 'Moon and spoon rhyme and so do dog and frog. Do moon and dog rhyme?'.
- Expose children to common, frequently used words such as the, am, here, etc. to help them build up a bank of sight words.
- Encourage children to:
  - identify letters that occur in their names
  - point to the first or last letter of a word
  - count the letters in a word
  - count the words in a sentence
  - match words with words in messages on the wall or blackboard
  - find other words around the room that begin with the same letter
  - draw attention to a long or short word.

Teaching Emphases

Use modelled and shared reading sessions to expose children to:

- the joy of reading
- strategies readers use, including:
  - having-a-go
  - reading common words such as the, a, was, have 'without thinking'
  - initial letter cues
- concepts of print:
  - directionality - left to right, and up/down
  - that a word can be written down
  - that a word is a unit of print with space either side
  - that a word is made up of letters
- conventions of print:
  - terminology such as word, letter
- sound and graphophonic relationships:
  - initial letters
  - Rhyming words
- word knowledge
  - a few frequently used words
  - some interesting words, long words and short words.

Context 2: Complementary Activities

Activities which reinforce concepts introduced in shared and modelled reading and writing offer children further opportunities to refine or consolidate an understanding or strategy which they are developing.

Such activities provide alternative and additional opportunities for children to learn in an environment that fosters enquiry, problem solving, experimentation and interaction.

Teaching Suggestions

- Teach children to play 'Lucky Letter Dip'. Children close eyes and select a letter from a container. They then have to find another one of those letters somewhere in the room.
- Teach names of the letters of the alphabet using alphabet rhymes and jingles, alphabet books, blocks and charts.
- Enable children to explore letter shapes using a variety of materials such as plasticine, coloured paper, wool, sawdust, sand, playdough, clay, pipe cleaners.
- Set up letter stepping stones - children can make up their own hopping and jumping games.
- Help children to play alphabet card games.
- Provide opportunities for children to identify any known letters in words around the classroom.
- Challenge children to find letters from their own names in other words.
- Encourage children to use letter cards, felt letters or magnetic letters to make words.
- Set up 'Fishing for Letters', e.g. 'How many 'b' letters can you catch?', 'Can you catch all the letters of your name?'
- Introduce children to simple Word Sorting (see *Spelling: Resource Book*, Chapter 4). Help children to cut out pictures of objects from magazines and newspapers and classify them according to the initial letters.
- Play 'Simon Says'.
- Say a sentence or phrase slowly and ask children to clap or put out a block for each word they hear.
- Chant children's names, clapping for each syllable.
- Play the game 'Whispers'. Children sit in a circle. Teacher whispers a word, phrase or sentence which is passed from child to child.
- Make up rhymes using children's names.
- Children complete known nursery rhymes by saying the missing word:
    'Humpty Dumpty sat on the wall
    Humpty Dumpty had a great_____'
    'Jack and Jill went up the _____'

- Play 'I Spy' in a very simplified form, e.g. 'I spy something that is brown, has four legs, goes 'woof' and its name starts with 'D''.
- Make up alliterative sentences which stem from the children's names, e.g.
    Marion makes mud pies
    Simon says shshshsh
    Peter paints pictures
    Dan draws dogs
    Lola likes lions
    Li likes lemons
    Jessica jumps like a jack-in-a-box.
- Take each child's name in turn and ask children to think of as many words as possible which start with that letter-sound.

Teaching Emphases

Complementary activities provide opportunities for children to refine and consolidate specific knowledge and understandings such as:
- understandings about words:
    - that a word is a unit of print with space either side
    - that a word is made up of letters
    - that a word can be segmented into syllables
    - that words can rhyme with each other
- knowledge of the alphabet:
    - letter names
    - that a letter has one name but can represent several sounds
- phonological awareness:
    - the sounds of words
    - that a word can be segmented into separate sounds
       the sounds of letters.

Context 3: Independent Writing

It is essential that children in the Preliminary Phase of spelling be given time and opportunity to 'write' independently in a whole range of different contexts every day. Children who are in the Role Play and Experimental Phases of writing and who are Preliminary spellers will only develop appropriately and progress into the next phase if they can apply their growing understandings independently through purposeful writing. Purposeful writing develops from and through scribble and approximations of adult writing. It is essential that children are given time and opportunity for experimentation. Children's writing will develop through a range of different types of scribble and approximations of letters to print, which shows they have made a connection between symbol and sound. If they are not able to write in their own way, but are constrained to produce 'good' writing through copying and producing 'proper' letters, they may produce a correct piece of work in the short term. They will not, however, be able to construct the essential understandings for themselves that will enable them to develop into competent and able readers, writers and spellers.

Classrooms are teeming with opportunities and reasons for writing. Some writing will emerge from play and some will be for real-life purposes and audiences. The more children write, the more they focus on print, and the ways in which they can use the written language for their own purposes. As they write they develop more effective strategies and construct deeper understandings about the writing and spelling process .

Teaching Suggestions

- Display and make available a range of resources such as:
  - An alphabet frieze
  - Charted stories, rhymes, children's news and other meaningful texts
  - Labels, word banks and lists constructed with the children
  - Alphabet books
  - A large and changing range of books of all types
  - Magnetic or felt letters
  - A children's blackboard and chalk
  - A Writing Table, with a variety of writing materials such as different kinds of paper, pencils, felt pens, paint.
  - 'The class shop'
    - note pad, pencils, signs 'shop open' or 'shop closed'
    - telephone and message book
    - magnetic letters, price tags and sale tickets
    - household articles that display labels, brands etc.
    - for sale' lists written by the children
    - magazines and newspaper clippings
    - posters
    - play money
  - 'The Doctor's Surgery'
    - an appointment book
    - telephone and pad
    - 'Doctor in' - 'Doctor out' sign
    - an alphabet or picture eye chart
    - post showing the human body and labelled parts
  - 'The Fire Station'
    - signs
    - 'Fire Station', 'EXIT', 'Alarm'
    - labelled map of classroom for locating 'fires'
    - a log book of fires
  - 'The Post Office'
    - note paper
    - envelopes and stamps
    - post box
    - post bag - letters for sorting
  - 'The Restaurant '
    - menus
    - order pads
    - bills
  - 'The Home Corner '
    - shopping lists
    - telephone book
    - names and addresses
    - recipe book
    - message board

- Encourage children to have-a-go at writing for themselves daily, from the time they begin pre-school. Display their 'writing' and accept it as it is. Ask children to read their writing so that they are aware of an audience.
- Encourage written responses to stories.
- Encourage children to write letters to people for real reasons. A 'translation' can be appended.
- Encourage children to use picture cards to record days of the week and weather patterns on charts, e.g. 'Today is Monday' 'It is sunny'.
- Encourage children to label their own writing and pictures.

Teaching Emphases

Children experiment with and apply understandings. These and many other writing contexts offer children opportunities to write for a wide range of purposes and audiences. Use these opportunities to assess if children:

- emulate what they have seen adults do
- work out how the written language relates to the spoken language
- experiment with concepts and conventions of print
- explore ways of representing words.

Children learn through problem solving, they learn to write by writing and to spell as they begin to represent words. When children are given opportunities to do so, they will apply and refine the understandings they are developing in shared and modelled reading and writing sessions.

Context 4: Modelled and Shared Writing

A wide range of different forms of writing can be undertaken by the teacher and shared with the children. The teacher shows how successful writers meet challenges by 'thinking aloud', solving problems and making decisions. Children learn how writers change and adapt texts to suit themselves, their purpose and their audience and how they cope with the challenge of representing words on paper.

Teaching Suggestions

- When the opportunity arises, model a thank-you letter in a whole class or small group situation.
- Brainstorm class instructions, e.g. 'How to feed the fish'
- Let the children help you print signs and labels, e.g. helpers chart, resource table labels.
- Scribe class rules suggested by children, e.g. 'We sit down when we eat our fruit.'
- Write messages in front of the children, e.g. 'I am writing a note to the cleaner to ask him to close the window.' or 'Please wash your hands after playtime'.
- Introduce a new song or poem to the class by writing it out in front of the children.
- Write recipes during a cooking session
- Create language experience books with the children.
- Involve children in shadow plays using the overhead projector. Introduce dialogue.
- Use children's names to label drawings, news items, storage units
- Be seen to be writing down reminder notes to self, parents and children
- Write simple messages to children and respond in writing to any written messages received.
- Make graphs of pets, families, toys, favourite colours, etc. Write a summary on the bottom of the graph, e.g. 'In our class we have more people with dogs than cats.'
- Involve children in self-awareness activities, e.g. record eye and hair colour, size of foot and hand or height of children on graphs labelled with names
- Make a large birthday card or chart on which the children's names and birthdays can be displayed.
- Write well known nursery rhymes on charts. Talk about the writing process as you do it.
- Write in front of the children repeating each word as it is written. Read through the text with the children, point to each word.
- Each day at a set time ask children to discuss something they have done during the session. Teacher scribes and then asks a child to illustrate the text. If this is done everyday it becomes a useful record of class events and experiences. It also provides a context for discussions about letters, words and concepts of print.

- Use the children's sentences to make meaningful sentence strips. The sentences may be written through scribing children's news. Children can read the sentence strips, matching spoken with written words. Strips can be organised into a sequence. Sentences can be cut up and children can realign words.
- Use a topic to develop a list of words which may be used in independent writing.
- With the children, make a list of words which they constantly encounter and need to write, this will form the basis of a sound sight vocabulary.

Teaching Emphases

Use modelled and shared writing sessions to expose children to:
- the importance of having-a-go at writing and spelling
- concepts of print:
  - that print and pictures are different and that the message is in the print
  - that print carries a constant message
  - directionality: left to right and top to bottom
  - that a word can be written down
  - that a word is a unit of print with space either side
  - that a word is made up of letters
  - terminology such as word, letters, sounds
  - initial letter sounds
  - that a letter can represent a range of sounds
  - the concept of rhyming words.

Context 5: Independent Reading

The classroom provides many opportunities and a wide range of purposes for children to read. It is when children are engaged in reading for themselves that they can come to grips with the concepts and conventions of print and the ways in which letters and words are represented. Children sometimes like to read peacefully by themselves, but they need to know that they are free to ask questions and discuss issues with others should the need arise.

Teaching Suggestions

- Create a print-rich environment by providing labels, signs, descriptions on murals, charts of poems, lists of known songs, helper's rosters, instructions, timetables, word banks.
- Provide a box of name cards so that children can mark the occasions for turns at helping at fruit time, feeding fish, tidying book shelves.
- Have an attractive reading corner that is always accessible to children, where children's favourite books, poems, songs, picture books and simple informational texts are always available.
- Provide an alphabet frieze in the classroom so that children can identify the letters of their names and other letters that are significant to them.
- Set up specific play centres representing familiar contexts such as the Bank, Post Office, Doctor's surgery, shop, restaurant, displaying appropriate reading materials.
- Set up a cooking corner, including:
  - cookery books
  - class recipe book
  - list of items used, e.g. pots, pans, spoons, knifes and ingredients
  - food charts
  - a list of duties
- Make use of messages around the room that provide information and are meaningful to the children, e.g. 'Swimming tomorrow' or 'Today is Thursday'
- Create a 'Song Box'. Print out songs on cards as they are taught. Use pictures to assist children to recognise a song. During mat sessions encourage children to select, and 'read' or sing songs from the box. Use this idea for the storage of poems and rhymes as well.
- Encourage children to read environmental print when on excursions.
- Have sessions when children can choose a book and 'read' it interactively with a friend.
- Put a different message on the blackboard everyday. Use the same sentence pattern until the children have assimilated it, e.g.
  - Monday - Today we are going to swim.
  - Tuesday - Today we are going to cook.
  - Wednesday - Today we are going to play sports. Draw a picture above the word which changes to enable the children to 'read' it for themselves.

Teaching Emphases

Children experiment with and apply understandings that they are developing. It is when children are interpreting print for themselves that they construct knowledge about the concepts and conventions of print and how words are represented in print.

Children need to have-a-go at reading independently to explore and refine the understandings they are gaining from shared and modelled reading and writing.

Their early experiences with books, environmental print and, above all, with their own names, leads them to realise that:

- print is constant
- the spoken language is made up of words
- words are represented by units of print with spaces in between them
- words are made up of letters
- letters represent the sounds they can hear in the words.

Children need to know that books and the wealth of meaningful print around the room provide resources for finding out how to spell words.

In their personal reading children work through and test their developing understandings. They need many opportunities to do this in motivating situations with time to think and talk.

Context 6: Sharing and Reflecting

Learning to stand back, reflect on and talk about what has been achieved and learned is important for everyone. Children need to be given time, opportunity and support as they think and talk about what they have learned. They need to be aware of their achievements and to be able to demonstrate and represent their learning to others in ways which make sense to them.

Teaching Suggestions

- Modelling the process of reflective thinking is essential. For instance, at the end of a modelled writing session, 'I enjoyed writing that letter and I think that, after having several tries, I managed to find the right words' or 'Some of the words I used were a bit dull, but I loved inventing that word *ragtagtattybag* and working out how to write it down'; or after shared reading, 'Well, we all enjoyed that story and I specially liked the page where the word BIG was written in such huge letters' or 'I thought it was fun when the giant kept saying 'Fi, Fi, Fo, Fum', I'm going to write a story about a giant dog that says 'Di, Di, Do, Dum''.
- Children can be given specific prompts such as, 'You made a really good list of things we need in the dressing-up box, Sandy. Can you tell us what you did when you wanted to write *hat*? … Can anyone else remember finding out how to write a word down?'
- Provide opportunities for specific reflection and reporting at the end of an activity. This need not involve the whole class, which could be very daunting.
  - Give children a few minutes to think about something they have enjoyed or puzzled over during the day. Ask them what happened and how they managed to do it.
  - Ask them to turn to the person next to them and tell that person about it. First one person has a talking turn and then the other.
  - Vary the context by modelling the same procedure using a puppet. Then let the children have a go at telling the puppet something they have done or learned during the session which made them feel good.
- Help children to take control of and responsibility for their learning by using the 'What I can do' check lists provided in this book.
- Create a large chart which will be displayed throughout the year. Chart children's contributions in pre-determined spaces, so that children can see that what they know is valued and that their individual discoveries gradually combine to create the whole picture of the spelling system.

Teaching Emphases

Modelling of reflective thinking and reporting can include:
- the attitudinal component of learning
  - feelings such as excitement, pleasure, apprehension
  - a sense of worth
  - a sense of achievement and pride
  - knowledge of successful learning
  - the value and importance of taking risks
- strategies being learned
  - having-a-go at representing words
  - looking for letters and words in environ-mental print
  - matching letters with an alphabet frieze
  - using the sounds and letters of own name or familiar words
  - matching letters and words in meaningful contexts
- knowledge and understanding
  - concepts of print
  - conventions of print
  - letter names
  - simple graphophonic relationships
  - rhyming words
  - segmenting words into syllables
  - recognising the different sounds in a word
  - a few very well used sight words.

Preliminary Spelling Phase

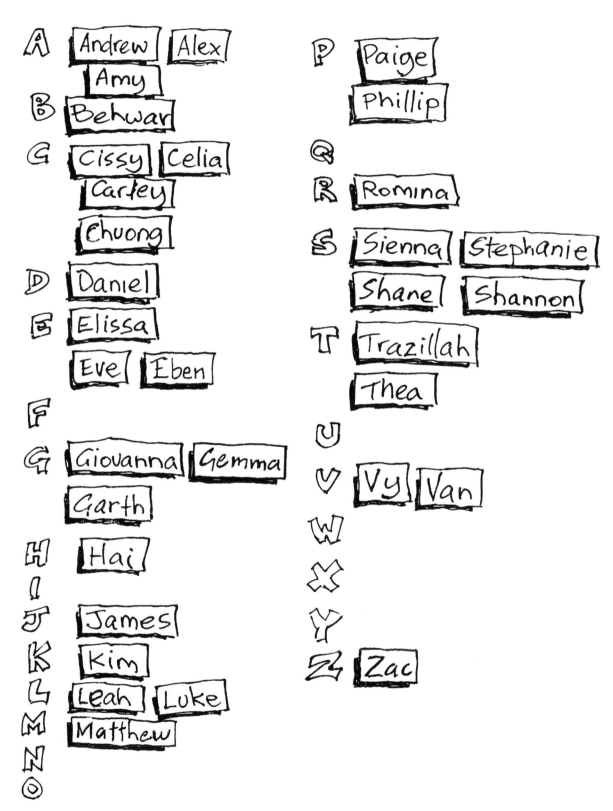

A classroom alphabet chart, which children can use to explore the initial sounds of their names and those of their friends. Children decided where to put their names.

For Parents

How can I help my child with spelling?

- Read favourite books again and again. Encourage children to join in and help turn the pages at the right time. Talk a lot about the pictures, but make it quite clear that the story, which stays the same every time, is read from the print and not the pictures.
- When you are reading stories, sometimes comment on interesting or unusual words, pointing and saying, for instance, 'What a long word!'
- Look at alphabet books with your child. Using letter names, talk about the letters and the sounds they make in relation to the pictures. Make connections with family names or objects in the room.
- Sing alphabet songs together. If you don't know any, make one up by singing the alphabet to a well known tune.
- Say nursery rhymes with your child and let him/her contribute the last word or phrase.
- Talk about print in the shops, street and on television. For instance, 'That says 'STOP' or 'No dogs' or 'EXIT''. Talk about print in advertisements or shop signs.
- Draw attention to your child's written name as often as you can. For instance, write the name in the front of books, help her/him write her/his name in birthday cards, label paintings etc.
- Draw attention to the initial sound of your child's name. Connect this with the initial letter.
- Encourage your child to recognise the first letter of his/her name when it appears as the first letter in other contexts, for instance, Sam might say, pointing to the S in STOP, 'That's my name' and you might reply 'Yes, That's S for Sam'.
- Put labels on things, for instance, 'Annabel's toy box'.
- Provide scrap paper and crayons or pencils. Encourage your child to draw and scribble. Show pleasure when she/he starts to make letter-like formations. When real letters start appearing, don't worry if they are mixed up with numerals, scribble or simulated letters. Display all their efforts and show them to friends. Value all early attempts to write, whatever form they take.
- Write notes, shopping lists, cards etc in front of your child, explaining what you are writing.
- Play games in the car, recognising the letters and numbers on the numberplates.
- When you go to the bank or post office, let your child 'fill in a form' while she/he waits for you.

Semi-Phonetic Spelling

In this phase children show developing understanding of sound-symbol relationships. Their spelling attempts show some evidence of sound-symbol correspondence. They may represent a whole word with one, two or three letters. In this, as in all phases of development children will be copying, recalling and inventing words. Children at this phase are able to copy letter by letter.

so   is g   to c   a s

someone is going to climb a slide

The writer:

- ◆ **uses left to right and top to bottom orientation of print**
- ◆ **relies on the sounds which are most obvious to him or her. This may be the initial sound, initial and final sounds, or initial, medial and final sounds, e.g. D (down), DN (down), DON (down), KT (kitten), WT (went), BAB (baby), LRFT (elephant)**
- ◆ **represents a whole word with one, two or three letters. Uses mainly consonants, e.g. KGR (kangaroo), BT (bit)**
- • uses an initial letter to represent most words in a sentence, e.g. s o i s g to c a s (Someone is going to climb a slide)
- • recognises some sound-symbol relationships in context, e.g. points to 'ship' and says 'sh' or recognises first letter of name
- • is willing to have a go at representing speech in print form
- • is confident to experiment with words
- • talks about what has been drawn, written
- • is keen to share written language discoveries with others

Semi-Phonetic Spelling Indicators

The writer:

◆ **uses left to right and top to bottom orientation of print**

◆ **relies on the sounds which are most obvious to him or her. This may be the initial sound, initial and final sounds, or initial medial and final sounds, e.g. D (down), DN (down), DON (down), KT (kitten), WT (went), BAB (baby), LRFT (elephant)**

◆ **represents a whole word with one, two or three letters. Uses mainly consonants, e.g. KGR (kangaroo), BT (bit)**

• uses an initial letter to represent most words in a sentence, e.g. s o i s g to c a s (Someone is going to climb a slide)

• uses letter names to represent sounds, syllables or words, e.g. AT (eighty)

• uses a combination of consonants with a vowel related to a letter name, e.g. GAM (game), MI (my)

• writes one or two letters for sounds, then adds random letters to complete the word, e.g. greim (grass), rdms (radio)

• begins to use some simple common letter patterns, e.g. th (the), bck (bike)

• uses a small bank of known sight words correctly

• recognises some sound-symbol relationships in context, e.g. points to 'ship' and says 'sh' or recognises first letter of name

• knows the letters of the alphabet by name

• recognises some words in context, e.g. 'That says 'dog''

• recognises rhyming words

• recognises and copies words in the environment

• leaves spaces between word-like letter clusters, e.g. I h bn sik (I have been sick)

• confuses words with objects they represent, e.g. 'Train is a long word, 'cos trains are long. Butterfly is a little word...'

• is willing to have-a-go at writing

• is confident to experiment with words

• talks about what has been drawn, written

• seeks response by questioning

• is keen to share written language discoveries with others.

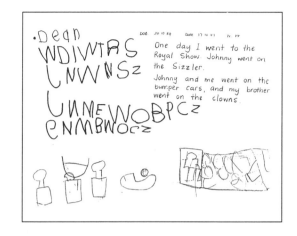

'I'm riding my bike'

Teaching Notes

In the Semi-Phonetic phase children begin to come to terms with the alphabetic system, as they realise that a sound can be represented by a written letter. Initially they may connect a spoken word, or part of it, with the sound of a letter name. For instance, a child spelt the word 'beach' 'BH' because the sound represented by 'bea...' is the same as the sound of the letter name B, and the 'ch' sound could be heard at the end of the letter name H. The sounds and letters of their own names are of great significance. These two factors form a scaffold around which children build their growing understandings.

It is essential that children in this phase continually encounter print in contexts that make sense to them; in the environment, in books, in letters, lists and notices. They need to develop a clear understanding that a word can be written down, that it is a unit of print with space either side, and that a written word is constant. Their understanding that a single word can be segmented into a sequence of sounds is beginning to develop. Children should be encouraged to experiment with writing whenever the opportunity arises, in play or real life. It is through experimentation and having-a-go that they construct and consolidate their developing understandings.

Major Teaching Emphases

Semi-Phonetic spellers need to be exposed to print in natural and meaningful contexts. They need opportunities to experiment with writing so they will develop understandings about print.

- ◆ **help children develop a stable concept of a word**
- ◆ **help children to hear different sounds in words**
- ◆ **help children develop the ability to segment spoken words into individual sounds**
- ◆ **help children to represent sounds heard in words with letters written in the order they are heard**
- ◆ **select high interest and high frequency words from children's reading and class writing to add to class word lists**
- ◆ **teach children that letter names are constant but the sounds they represent vary**
- ◆ **provide many opportunities for children to explore and identify sound-symbol relationships in meaningful contexts**
- • develop and use alphabetical lists
- • select high interest and high frequency words from children's reading and class writing to add to class word lists

At all phases:

- ◆ **model writing in a variety of contexts**
- ◆ **encourage students to reflect on their spelling strategies**
- ◆ **encourage children to reflect on their understandings, gradually building a complete picture of the spelling system**

◆ **ensure that students have opportunities to write for a variety of audiences and purposes**
◆ **encourage students to take risks and have-a-go at spelling words they need to write.**

◆ *Entries in bold are considered critical to the children's further development.*

Creating Effective Classroom Contexts

The following teaching sequence illustrates how a strategy such as syllabification and concepts such as sound-symbol relationships, the concept of a word and rhyming words, can be introduced and threaded through the day using the six major classroom contexts previously described (modelled and shared reading, complementary activities, independent writing, modelled and shared writing, independent reading, sharing and reflecting sessions). Activities will be structured for individuals, small groups or the whole class, according to the children's needs and the demands of context and purpose and audience.

Modelled and Shared Reading

A story such as *The Gingerbread Man* could be chosen for a shared book session. In a subsequent reading all the children can chant the refrain:
'*Run, run, run as fast as you can,*
You can't catch me, I'm the Gingerbread man.'
A focus will be placed on the rhyming words.
At another time a focus may be on a specific grapho-phonic relationship. Children scan the text and search the room for words with a specific initial letter. If a child's name begins with the letter, this will be duly noted. These words will be charted and will become the springboard for subsequent activities when the letter will be explored by the children.

Complementary Activities

Children can look for rhyming words. List them. If children find a word with the same letter pattern but which sounds different, congratulate them and start another list.
The class can make nonsense sequences using children's names, e.g. 'Kay, Bay, Cay, Day', 'Philip, Billip, Cillip, Dillip', Children can chant and 'clap the syllables' of the names when they are being invented. 'Nonsense Names' can then be written on cards and used for sorting purposes. Some sorting criteria could be: rhyme, initial letter, 'number of claps'. This will give children an opportunity to apply their knowledge of the alphabet, of rhyme and of syllabification.
It is important that the construction of word banks is on-going. Give children time. Praise them for small discoveries and enable them to modify or add to these over time. Encourage them to construct a rule from their findings, e.g. 'Does G always make a hard sound if it has an R in front of it or after it?' The possibilities are endless!

Independent Writing

As a result of their shared reading session, children will want to attempt their own text innovations or to retell the story in their own way. The sharing and talk which has preceded this session will be continued as children meet the challenge of capturing words and representing them in print at their own level of development. The charts and text innovations which are displayed in the room provide a rich source of information for children to draw on. There will be much interaction as they help each other and thus clarify their understandings. The teacher will observe what strategies children are using as they write, how they apply their knowledge of sound-symbol relationships and whether they are beginning to 'sound' words into viable syllables.

Modelled and Shared Writing

The children's understanding of the concept of a word can be extended by carrying out a text innovation on the refrain from *The Gingerbread Man*.
The innovation could focus, for instance, on the replacement of *run* with a range of different words. Children enjoy suggesting verbs such as *skip, hop, fly, jump* etc. This activity can help develop the concept of syllabification. Children will see that all the words which 'fit' the rhythm consist of one block of sound and not two or three. To make this point, encourage children to 'clap the sounds'. Then ask them to 'clap the sounds' that are made when words such as *hurry* or *somersault* are substituted. They will find out that the rhythm is disrupted. This aspect of the activity helps them to segment words into blocks of sound, a crucial skill which needs to be acquired at this phase of development.

Modelled Writing

The teacher may choose to model the writing of an alternative text innovation. This could focus on rhyme. It is much easier for children to recognise a rhyming word than to produce one, which is why the teacher needs to control this writing session. The refrain could be changed, for instance, to:
'Run, run, run, I'm chasing a rat,
You can't catch me, I'm the gingerbread cat'.
Begin to model early editing strategies in a very low-key manner, e.g. 'Oops, I should have put that on a new line' or 'Oh dear, you can't read that, can you? I'd better write it again'.

Independent Reading

There will be many times during the day when the
concepts introduced in the shared reading and shared and
modelled writing sessions are reinforced and further
developed as children re-read books like *The Gingerbread
Man* for themselves, read-along with a tape, or read some
of the innovations which have been placed in the reading
corner. Don't forget to write new discoveries on the class
chart.

Sharing and Reflecting

Each experience provides an opportunity for reflecting on
what has been learned. When children have set out to
meet a challenge and solve a problem, they are acutely
aware of their discoveries. Their reporting will tend to be
centred on time and place, e.g. 'When I was looking for the
book on snails I suddenly saw the alphabet book, so I...'
Children can be encouraged to keep a list of one or two
things they have learned that day. The list may be
primitive, but it will provide a context for expressing
through a word, a picture or a letter, something which has
held meaning for them. All discoveries can be written on a
large wall chart which is initially blank, but is gradually
filled up as the children discover more and more. In this
way all contributions will be valued and children will
develop a sense of how the whole jig-saw of spelling fits
together (see illustration on page 52).
Children can also use the 'What I can do' check lists
provided at the end of this book.

Integrated and On-going Learning

The series of teaching activities described above
demonstrates how concepts and strategies can be
introduced, followed through, extended and consolidated
in ways which make sense to children and give them
control over their learning. The teacher has made the links
between context, text and process clear to the children.
The movement which has taken place from the whole to a
specific focus and then back to the whole again supports
and enhances learning and enables children to generalise
beyond the immediate activity into a range of different
contexts. Once again, it can clearly be seen that structured
periods of reflection help children become aware of and
control their learning.

Context 1: Modelled and Shared Reading

Modelled and shared reading continue to provide contexts which enable children to gain insights into and access the reading process. Their developing understandings will be reflected in their writing and in their spelling. Shared reading enables children to interact with print and with other readers in exciting, supportive and purposeful ways. Modelled reading gives them insights into the strategies readers use to create meaning.

Modelled and Shared Reading provides one of the most powerful contexts for productive teaching and learning about the way that written language works, the processes readers use and the strategies writers employ.

Teaching Suggestions

- Continue to read a wide range of texts such as poetry, riddles, narrative and informational texts. Offer children opportunities to identify letters/letter patterns/grapho-phonic relationships in context.
- Share a range of alphabet books with children.
- Read stories that provide identifiable structures and have repetitive sequences, i.e. cumulative (The House that Jack Built), circular (There's a Hole in My Bucket), traditional narrative frameworks (fairy stories) and traditional stories with a refrain such as in *Billy Goats Gruff*. This will help children, through repetition and confirmation, to focus on words and features of words.
- Give children simple written directions that use common sight words (in, on, the, have, put etc) in a meaningful context such as in art and craft.
- Read pamphlets, posters, signs with the children. Emphasise their functions and draw attention to specific features of words and the way they are presented.
- Retell favourite stories, poems, rhymes using felt board, overhead projector and puppets to emphasise and highlight features of words.
- Involve children in chanting:
  - favourite poems and rhymes
  - health and safety rhymes
  - frame sentences, such as
  - I like fruit/cookies/books/outings
  - I hate spiders/marzipan/wearing shoes
  - I can jump high
  - I can run fast…
  Draw attention to the sounds of language, to rhythm and rhyme and to similarities and differences. Children will enjoy having their own copies of texts that have been created by the group.

- Use the blackboard or easel to write clues about characters or objects in stories for the children to solve:
  - My name starts with sp…
  - I am hairy
  - I frighten people
  - I have eight legs
  - Remember, my name starts with sp…
  Encourage children to guess the answer after each clue is unveiled.
- Ask children to identify words from a text which have the same sound. Record the words on cards. Group the words according to (1) sound patterns, and (2) visual patterns.
- Read tongue twisters with the children. Have them identify the focus sound and make up their own tongue twisters.
- After reading a text with the children, ask them to identify all the words beginning with or containing a letter such as 's'. Then classify the words according to the sound represented by the letter, e.g. saw, step; is, was; sheep, shop.

Teaching Emphases

Use shared and modelled reading sessions to expose children to:

- the joy of reading
  - sharing written language discoveries with others
- concepts of print
  - the understanding that a word is made up of units of sound
  - the understanding that letter names are constant, but the sounds they represent will vary
- conventions of print
  - terminology relating to factors such as letters of the alphabet, words
- graphophonic relationships
  - the sounds represented by initial, medial and final letters
  - the segmentation of words into phonemes which are represented by appropriate letters in sequence
- sounds of words
  - rhyme, rhythm and repetition
  - onomatopoeia
  - the segmentation of words into syllables
- words
  - word banks of high interest and high frequency words from familiar texts
  - common visual patterns such as th, sh, …ing
- strategies
  - initial letter cues
  - having-a-go
  - prior knowledge
  - semantic cues.

Context 2: Complementary Activities

It is important that children are given opportunities to focus on and practise aspects of spelling that they have been exposed to in shared and modelled reading and writing sessions. They may also need to explore further an understanding that has been engaging their attention as they read and write independently. Complementary activities can provide motivating contexts that extend and consolidate learning. Children need to see the links between such activities and the 'real' reading and writing that they are undertaking every day.

Teaching Suggestions

- Play 'What Comes Next?' (see *Spelling: Resource Book*, Chapter 4).
- Construct 'Secret Messages' (see *Spelling: Resource Book*, Chapter 3).
- Play 'Change a Letter'. Start with a simple three or four letter word and see how many different words can be made by changing one letter at a time, e.g. bin/pin/pan/pat/put/pet/get...
- Play 'Word Sorts' using a range of different criteria such as first letter, final letter, number of letters, rhyming words, one or two syllables (see *Spelling: Resource Book*, Chapter 4).
- Use 'sound frames' to help children to hear the order of sounds in words:
  - choose two syllable words and ask children to clap for each chunk of sound they hear.
  - increase the number of syllables to three or four when the children are ready
  - ask children to put a block on the table for every chunk of sound they hear
  - draw boxes for sound segments heard
  - help children put appropriate letters in the boxes.
- Use 'story cards' of a familiar story with pictures and text that can be used for text reconstruction activities.
- Make letter shape mobiles. Cut out letter shapes, e.g. C, and hang words from the shape that start with that letter, e.g. cat, call, chair, circus, Cindy, Chuck, chicken, comb etc.
- Make strings of words starting with the same letter or digraph.
- Play 'Change a Word'. Write the words of a well known nursery rhyme on a large chart. Sing or chant the rhyme several times so that children can 'hear' the rhythm. Underline a word that could be replaced. Cover the word and ask children to suggest a substitute.

Teaching Emphases

Complementary activities provide opportunities for children to refine and consolidate specific knowledge and understandings such as:
- understandings about words:
  - that a word is a unit of print with space either side
  - that a word is made up of letters
  - that a word can be segmented into syllables
  - that words can rhyme with each other
- knowledge of the alphabet:
  - letter names
  - that a letter has one name but can represent several sounds
- phonological awareness:
  - the sounds of words
  - that a word can be segmented into separate sounds
  - that a word can be 'sounded out' in sequential segments
  - the sounds of letters.

Context 3: Independent Writing

Independent writing continues to provide one of the most powerful vehicles for applying, clarifying and further developing understandings and strategies essential to reading, writing and spelling. It is when children are writing independently that teachers are able to observe what they do. Children's spelling attempts provide visible evidence of their current understandings. The more children write, the more they focus on print, and the ways in which they can use the written language for their own purposes. As they write they develop more effective strategies and construct deeper understandings about the process of representing words in print. They are able to apply their understandings in a range of contexts and to use spelling as a tool for writing. Classrooms which encourage children to experiment and take risks and which give them freedom to express themselves through the spoken and written word provide contexts in which children achieve their potential as active and effective learners.

Teaching Suggestions

- Establish a writing table or corner. Maintain interest by adding new writing implements and different paper. Leave 'secret messages' to attract children. Sometimes have a special focus like 'book week'. Respond in writing to children's messages, reflecting back to them conventional spellings of words they have used.
- Provide a class letterbox and encourage children to write letters to you and to each other. Post letters yourself. Ensure that children receive answers to their letters. Model correct spelling of words they have used in your replies.
- Set up a suggestion box. Encourage children to write about what they would like to do.
- Put writing materials in existing areas such as the news table and maths corner.
- Place writing materials on the science table so that children can label their contributions and write about them.
- Provide a message board.
- Provide a table and writing materials in the book corner so that children can write comments and reviews on books read.
- Brainstorm word lists related to class topics under study.
- Provide opportunities for children to write shopping lists for cooking sessions.
- Make language experience books for the reading corner.
- Make re-tell books and books of text innovations.
- Encourage children to write in speech bubbles and write captions and titles for pictures.

Teaching Emphases

Children experiment with and apply understandings. These and many other writing contexts offer children opportunities to write for a wide range of purposes and audiences, applying their developing understandings about the spelling system.

Children use these opportunities to:
- take risks
- experiment with and apply strategies they have encountered in shared and modelled reading and writing
- further develop their concept of a word
- apply their developing knowledge of the alphabet
- further explore sound-symbol relationships
- use high interest and high frequency words they have encountered in texts
- experiment with the segmentation of words into individual sequential sounds
- begin to apply syllabification strategies.

Context 4: Modelled and Shared Writing

A wide range of different forms of writing are undertaken by the teacher and shared with the children. The teacher shows how successful writers meet challenges by 'thinking aloud', solving problems and making decisions. Children learn that writers change and adapt texts and choose words to suit themselves, their purpose and their audience. They need to learn more about the strategies writers use to represent their chosen words in print.

Teaching Suggestions

- Continue to read many different types of text with the children, exposing them to a wide vocabulary across a variety of contexts.
- Share a range of alphabet books with the children
- Compose a group story with the children. Teacher scribes each child's contribution. Talk about interesting words.
- Chain writing—the teacher starts a sentence, breaks off after two words, hands the chalk to a child who writes the next two and so on.
- Scribe the children's language:
  - to describe items of equipment
  - to describe children's constructions
  - to provide directions for using equipment
  - to describe group work.
  This will expose children to subject-specific words and to basic sight words.
- Scribe children's news to make a class news book.
- Write accounts and reports of excursions, incidents and talks by visitors.
- Make class photograph books with appropriate captions.
- Make big books of original stories, informational texts or retells.
- When talking about words or letters in context make sure that it is clear to the children which unit you are talking about by circling the letter or the whole word.
- Talk about the spelling of words as they are written, i.e. 'Jump has four letters, j - u - m - p'.
- Substitute character names with names of children and place names with local names.
- Carry out oral close activities.
- Read back sentences dictated by children. Children then read the sentence. Create sentence strips for sequencing. Cut sentence strips into individual words for word study activities.
- Ask children to identify words from a text with the same sound. Accept all suggestions regardless of visual patterns. Record the words and then ask the children to group the words according to visual patterns.

- Develop activities from texts that are being written such as identifying and classifying all the sounds that are represented by a letter, e.g. 's' - saw, trials, sheep.
- Construct a class dictionary from words in jointly constructed texts, emphasising alphabetical order.
- Select high frequency words from written texts to add to class word bank.
- Model some simple editing and proofing strategies as part of the writing process, without drawing special attention to them.

Teaching Emphases

Use modelled and shared writing sessions to expose children to:
- the importance of having-a-go at writing
- conventions of print:
  - terminology such as word, letter, sound, pattern
  - the use of basic punctuation such as full stops and speech marks, exclamation marks
  - alphabetical order
- sounds, symbols and words :
  - initial letter sounds
  - that letter names are constant, but the sounds they represent will vary
  - that a letter can represent a range of sounds
  - that a word can be segmented into individual sounds
  - syllabification.

Context 5: Independent Reading

The classroom provides many opportunities and a wide range of purposes for children to read. It is when children are engaged in reading for themselves that they can come to grips with the concepts and conventions of print and the ways in which sounds and words are represented. It is when they are reading independently that they further develop the meaning-making strategies they have encountered in shared and modelled reading sessions. Children sometimes like to read peacefully by themselves, but they need to know that they are free to ask questions and discuss issues with others should the need arise.

Teaching Suggestions

- The reading corner continues to be a much used area. Materials are constantly updated. Children may wish to share books and magazines from home with their friends for a period of time. Such material is highly valued and looked after with care. It may be possible to arrange for a consignment of books from the library to be changed each week. Very often these books will reflect a topic which is currently engaging the attention of the children. Comments on books or lists of books others might like to read can be contributed by children for others to read. The reading corner is constantly enriched by the addition of stories and informational texts written in shared writing sessions.
- Art and Craft lessons provide a rich context for reading, as children follow simple instructions. Subject areas such as science, social studies and mathematics provide a range of different forms of text which children can explore. Children are continually exposed to commonly used words which form the basis of their sight vocabulary.
- A high value can be placed on reading at home if time is set aside for children to share library books, 'old' books which their parents read as children, or any other interesting reading material they have come across.
- It is also important to make regular time available in class for quiet individual reading or paired or group reading.

Teaching Emphases

Children experiment with and apply understandings.

It is when children are constructing meaning from print for themselves that they extend their knowledge of the concepts and conventions of print and of the range of strategies readers use to make meaning.

Children need to read independently so that they can explore and refine the understandings they are gaining from shared and modelled reading and writing.

It is in their personal reading that children apply, consolidate and extend their developing understandings. They learn from experience that readers use a range of strategies for a variety of reasons. They need many opportunities to read in motivating situations with time to reflect and interact. It is self-motivated reading which fosters and perpetuates the desire to read and the knowledge that reading is intensely satisfying.

Context 6: Sharing and Reflecting

At this phase children are becoming more able to tell others about the discoveries they are making each day as they read and write. They know that their reports will be valued and their insights discussed with interest. At the end of each day it may be helpful to talk about the special event or achievement they will tell their family about when they get home. Sometimes it may be useful to write something down so that it does not get forgotten.

Teaching Suggestions

- Encourage children to keep very simple Journals that consist largely of isolated words or drawings. Children will enjoy looking back through the pages and trying to remember what meanings they were trying to express.
- Children can also be helped to monitor their learning through the 'What I can do' check lists provided. These can provide a focal point for conferences with the teacher.
- It is important to continue to model the process of reflective thinking. For instance, when sharing the writing of a letter to parents, say 'I can't remember what date it is. I'll have to go and look on the calender and find out', or 'I always forget how to spell 'practice', I never know whether it has an 's' or a 'c', I'll have to look in my dictionary.'
- Children can be given specific prompts such as, 'You made some very good labels for the science table, Melissa. Can you tell us how you knew how to spell the words?'
- Provide opportunities for specific reflection and reporting at the end of an activity. This need not involve the whole class, but could be carried out with small groups.
  - Give children a few minutes to think about something they have enjoyed or puzzled over during the day. Ask them what happened and how they managed to do it.
  - Ask them to turn to the person next to them and tell that person about it. First one person has a talking turn and then the other.
- Continue to add categories of words to the large chart which is displayed throughout the year. Chart children's contributions as they are offered. It may not be possible to write more than one prototype on the actual chart, but lists can be appended which include children's suggestions, so that children can see their discoveries are valued. When the appended lists get too big, words can be transferred into personal dictionaries to enable a new list to take shape.

Teaching Emphases

Modelling of reflective thinking and reporting can include:
  - feelings such as excitement, pleasure, apprehension
  - a sense of achievement and pride
  - knowledge of successful learning
  - understanding the value and importance of taking risks

and discussion of strategies such as:
  - having-a-go at representing words
  - using word banks as a resource for spelling
  - looking for words in familiar texts
  - applying developing graphophonic understandings
  - extending the store of sight words that can be used 'without thinking'
  - applying knowledge of rhyming words
  - segmenting words into syllables
  - recognising the different sounds in a word in sequence
  - a few very well used sight words.

Semi-Phonetic Spelling Phase

A B C D E F G H I J K L M N O P Q R S T U V W X Y Z

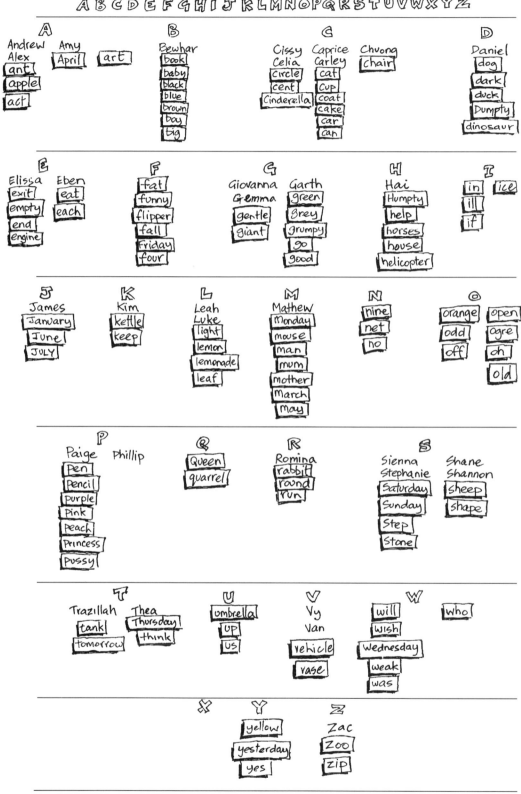

A
Andrew
Alex
Amy
ant
apple
act
April
art

B
Bewhar
book
baby
black
blue
brown
boy
big

C
Cissy
Celia
circle
cent
Cinderella
Caprice
Carley
cat
cup
coat
cake
car
can
Chuong
chair

D
Daniel
dog
dark
duck
Dumpty
dinosaur

E
Elissa
exit
empty
end
engine
Eben
eat
each

F
fat
funny
flipper
fall
Friday
four

G
Giovanna
Gemma
gentle
giant
Garth
green
grey
grumpy
go
good

H
Hai
Humpty
help
horses
house
helicopter

I
in
ill
if
ice

J
James
January
June
JULY

K
Kim
kettle
keep

L
Leah
Luke
light
lemon
lemonade
leaf

M
Mathew
Monday
mouse
man
mum
mother
March
may

N
nine
net
no

O
orange
odd
off
open
ogre
oh
old

P
Paige
Phillip
Pen
Pencil
purple
Pink
Peach
Princess
Pussy

Q
Queen
quarrel

R
Romina
rabbit
round
run

S
Sienna
Stephanie
Saturday
Sunday
Step
Stone
Shane
Shannon
sheep
shape

T
Trazillah
tank
tomorrow
Thea
Thursday
think

U
umbrella
up
us

V
Vy
Van
vehicle
vase

W
will
wish
Wednesday
weak
was
who

X

Y
yellow
yesterday
yes

Z
Zac
Zoo
zip

Children will add words to the class alphabet chart (see Preliminary Spelling Chart on page 36) as they discover them in books or environmental print. Alphabet lists should be displayed at child-height in the classroom.

For Parents

How can I help my child with spelling?

- Sometimes point to words as you read to your child, but do not interrupt the flow of the story unless the child asks a question. Comment on long words, short words, interesting words. Comment on the special features of these words. When you talk about a word, *circle* it with your finger. If you *point* at a word the child might confuse the word with the letter your finger is pointing at.
- Borrow a set of magnetic letters from the toy library and encourage your child to play with them, making her/his name or any other words.
- Continue to share your writing with your child on every possible occasion: when noting telephone messages, making shopping lists, filling in forms, writing letters or cards etc.
- Encourage your child to write on every possible occasion. Give him/her paper when you are writing so that she/he can write beside you. Make real reasons for writing such as greeting cards, letters, lists, messages etc. Always accept and value the writing and use it for the intended purpose.
- Always encourage your child to have-a-go at spelling; only give concrete help when it is demanded.
- Show amazement and delight when your child uses the initial letters or clusters of two or three letters when writing words. Do not correct the child, but value the approximation. If possible model the correct spelling in context. For instance, if the child writes on a picture 'I MrI My BCK' you can write 'I like to see you riding your bike'.
- If your child is trying to learn a word, help by:
  - encouraging him/her to have-a-go at spelling it first, to see how much of the word he/she already knows;
  - point out that she/he knows a lot about the word already, so she/he will only have to learn (2) letters;
  - use the 'look - cover - write - check' routine, stressing that the 'look' is for focusing on the unknown letters. For instance, if the child has spelled 'went' as 'we', the only bit that has to be learned is 'we<u>nt</u>'.
- Play *I spy with my little eye…*
- Continue to play numberplate games in the car, thinking of words which start with the letters.
- Continue to make attractive paper, note pads and pencils available to your child. If possible create a little writing table for his/her own use.
- Help your child to use a simple picture dictionary.

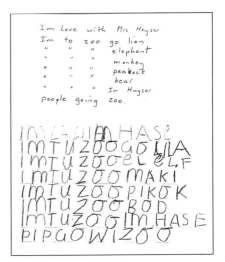

I'm love with Mrs Heyser
I'm to zoo go lion
I'm to zoo go elephant
I'm to zoo go monkey
I'm to zoo go peacock
I'm to zoo go bear
i'm to zoo I'm Heyser
People going zoo

I went to see a crane at school.

early Yer 1

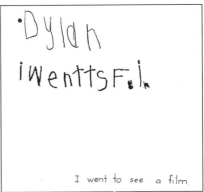

I went to see a film.

Phonetic Spelling

In this phase writers are able to provide an almost perfect match between letters and sounds. Letters are chosen on the basis of sound often without regard for conventional letter patterns. Spelling attempts are meaningful and becoming more like standard spelling. There is often evidence of self-constructed rules that may not conform to adult rules. Writers copy, recall and construct words according to their current understandings. They use rote recall for an increasing number of words.

Anna and Diana and the Lost Snowdrop

One day Anna and Diana, the twins, was playing in their garden when they heard a little voice, 'Help me, please'. Then they saw it was a little snowdrop. She had her little foot stuck between two large rocks. 'What's your name, little snowdrop?', asked Diana. 'Snowy' she said. A witch was chasing me and I got lost.', she said 'Then I slipped and fell.' There was a silence. Then Anna said 'You could stay with us.'

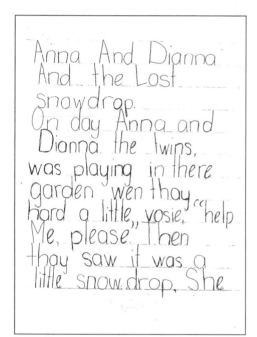

The writer:

◆ **chooses letters on the basis of sound without regard for conventional spelling patterns, e.g. wen (when), wich (witch), lage (large)**
◆ **sounds out and represents all substantial sounds in a word, e.g. roks (rocks), sad (said), silas (silence), anathe (another), aftrwoods (afterwards), siclon (cyclone), spidr (spider), isgrem (icecream), necst (next), peepl (people)**
◆ **develops particular spellings for certain sounds often using self-formulated rules, e.g. thay (they), stay**
• confuses short vowel sounds, e.g. hard (heard)
• sometimes omits one letter of a two letter blend or digraph, e.g. lage (large)
• usually spells commonly used sight words correctly, e.g. in, she, little, please, two, name
• uses some known patterns in words, e.g. ...ing, th..., sh..., nght (night)
• is beginning to use syllabification for spelling longer words, e.g. snowdrop, garden
• identifies and uses knowledge of similar sounding words, e.g. stay, thay (they)
• applies knowledge which has been gained from reading and words encountered in books, e.g. lost, twins, little, pirate, ship
• is willing to have-a-go at spelling
• sees self positively as a writer and speller.

Phonetic Spelling Indicators

The Writer:

- ◆ **chooses letters on the basis of sound without regard for conventional spelling patterns, e.g. kaj (cage), tabl (table), birgla (burglar), vampia (vampire), pepl (people), sum (some), bak (back)**
- ◆ **sounds out and represents all substantial sounds in a word e.g. ktn (kitten), wacht (watched), anathe (another), aftrwoods (afterwards), siclon (cyclone), spidr (spider), isgrem (icecream), necst (next), peepl (people)**
- ◆ **develops particular spellings for certain sounds often using self-formulated rules, e.g. becoz (because)/woz (was), wher (were)/whas (was), dor (door)/sor (saw)/mor (more), hape (happy)/ fune (funny), poot (put)/wood (would)**
- substitutes incorrect letters for those with similar pronunciation, e.g. oshan (ocean), nacher (nature), wold (world), heard (herd), disobays (disobeys), consert (concert), butiful (beautiful), tuched (touched), daw (door), tresher (treasure), thort (thought)
- adds an incorrect vowel after a correct vowel or consonant, e.g. hait (hat), derum (drum), miu (my), fiene (fine), saeid (said), beofore (before), seing (sing)
- represents past tense in different ways according to the sounds heard, e.g. stopt (stopped), watcht (watched), livd (lived)
- uses the letter 'r' to represent a syllable, e.g. watr (water), mothr (mother)
- confuses short vowel sounds, e.g. pell (pill), yallow (yellow), u (a), pan (pen), lat (let), sow (saw)
- sometimes omits one letter of a two letter blend or digraph, e.g. fog (frog), mik (milk), leve (leave), plak (plank)
- still uses some letter name strategies e.g. awa (away), exellnt (excellent), mit (might), lrst (last), cav (cave)
- creates some words by combining known sight words and patterns e.g. apreesheeight (appreciate), jenyouwine (genuine), MaThursday (Mother's Day)
- usually spells commonly used sight words correctly, e.g. in, has, his, he, my, the, here
- uses some known patterns in words, e.g. ...ing, th..., sh..., nght (night)
- is beginning to use syllabification for spelling longer words, e.g. telefon (telephone), butufl (beautiful). Some syllables may be omitted.
- identifies and uses knowledge of similar sounding words
- experiments with spelling words in different ways
- applies knowledge which has been gained from reading and words encountered in books, e.g. pirate, ship

- is beginning to use simple homonyms and homophones correctly, e.g. wind, read, park, their/ there, one/won, for/four, too/to
- is willing to have-a-go at spelling
- sees self positively as a writer and speller.

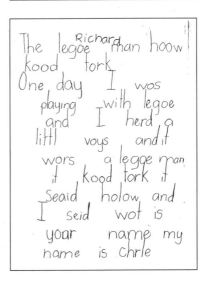

Teaching Notes

Children's spelling at this phase is logical and is very largely the outcome of their understanding of the relationships between letters and sounds. This understanding may not yet be the same as that of adults. Children's writing can be understood by other if it is read phonetically, although conventional connections may not always be made between letters and sounds. A typical example of unconventional spelling that could be related directly to logical thinking was provided by a little girl whose teacher was called 'Mrs Law'. This child consistently spelt 'door' as 'daw', 'more' as 'maw', 'pour' as 'paw' and 'saw' as 'saw'.

Phonetic spellers have also acquired a large bank of words that they can read, write and spell 'without thinking'.

It is crucial that children in this phase are encouraged to write spontaneously across a wide range of contexts so that they have many opportunities to try out and apply their understandings, gradually refining them in the light of all their encounters with print. If children feel that their spelling must be correct they will learn by rote rather than by constructing rules and will often restrict their use of words to the 'safe' vocabulary that they already know.

The emphasis in teaching at this stage focuses on categorising and classifying words according to spelling patterns. There should also be continued emphasis on building up a systematic view of spelling, i.e. letters can represent different sounds depending on context or place in the word—a sound can be represented by more than one letter or letters.

There is also a need to teach children to think about meaning as a strategy, particularly with inflected words, e.g. jump-jumped. It is appropriate at this stage to introduce strategies that will help children to identify critical features of words, i.e. differentiating characteristics.

Major Teaching Emphases

Phonetic spellers should be exposed to a wide variety of printed materials to provide data from which (at their own pace) they can draw new conclusions about spelling.

◆ **teach writers to look for visual patterns and common letter sequences in words**
◆ **teach writers to identify critical features of words (i.e. differentiating characteristics)**
◆ **continue to emphasise the building up of a systematic view of spelling with emphasis on the way:**
  (a) letters can represent different sounds depending on context or place in the word
  (b) a sound can be represented by more than one letter or letters
◆ **teach writers to think about meaning as a strategy**

- ◆ **continue the development of word banks by incorporating theme, topic, high frequency and interesting words as they arise**
- ◆ **introduce proof-reading strategies**
- • continue to explore and identify sound-symbol relationships
- • categorise and classify words according to spelling patterns
- • develop and use alphabetical lists
- • ensure that students have access to a wide range of reading materials on many topics

At all phases:
- ◆ **model writing in a variety of contexts**
- ◆ **encourage students to reflect on their spelling strategies**
- ◆ **encourage children to reflect on their understandings, gradually building a complete picture of the spelling system**
- ◆ **ensure that students have opportunities to write for a variety of audiences and purposes**
- ◆ **encourage students to take risks and have-a-go at spelling words they need to write**

◆ *Entries in bold are considered critical to the children's further development.*

Creating Effective Classroom Contexts

The following teaching sequence illustrates how concepts such as meaning and critical features of words and strategies such as applying knowledge of common letter patterns and sound-symbol relationships, can be introduced and threaded through the day using the six major classroom contexts of shared and modelled reading, complementary activities, shared and modelled writing, independent reading, independent writing and sharing and reflecting sessions. Activities are structured for individuals, small groups or the whole class, according to the children's needs and the demands of context and purpose and audience.

Shared Reading

An informational text, e.g. on birds, could be used for a shared reading session. The text might present children with some technical terms which they have not yet encountered, such as *fertile* and *incubate*. This would provide an opportunity for children to have-a-go at finding out the meaning of unknown words, such as:

- reading the text to see if the meaning is explicitly defined
- talking about the word to discover any links with other known words
- reading on or reading back to see if the meaning is implicit in the text.

Letter patterns arising from the text, e.g. 'hatch' could be explored (witch, fetch, catch, match...).

Complementary Activities

Letter patterns could form the focus of a Word Sleuth activity (see *Spelling: Resource Book* Chapter 3). For instance, the children could find words with *ea* in them, like 'beak'. They might come up with words such as *pearl, seal, each, endeavour* and many others. They can then classify them into sound categories. Children can continue to add to the list throughout the term.

A natural extension of this activity could be to focus on one of the sounds represented by *ea* in one of the categories, e.g. *ea* as in beak , and search for all the words containing this sound but using different letter patterns, for instance, peep, mete; or *ea* as in seal - peel; or as in pearl - hurl, girl. These words can be used for 'Snap' If children are having problems with reversals, play the game *What Comes Next*, which is described in the *Spelling: Resource Book* in Chapter 4.

Modelled and Shared Writing

The teacher might model the construction of a simple skeleton outline, encouraging children to brainstorm structure and content.

Children may notice the *ea* pattern in *beak* and *feathers* and that the words sound different.

Take any opportunities which arise to model editing and proof-reading skills.

If it is possible to incubate eggs in the classroom, a class diary could be kept and reports written on the process. The children can compile a glossary of technical terms.

HABITAT	FOOD	MOVEMENT	DESCRIPTION
NESTS TREES WATER	SEEDS BERRIES FLIES WORMS	FLY HOP RUN SWIM	TWO LEGS BEAK FEATHERS

Independent Reading

Children can carry out research, using suitable texts from the library. They can be encouraged to look for key words that have been identified in the shared reading session. With assistance they can use a structured overview to guide their reading and assist their comprehension. If they encounter words that they do not know, they can have-a-go at trying to find their meaning then look in the dictionary. These words can be noted and later shared with others. Extended word lists can be developed. They can be encouraged to find words with similar patterns to those that have been dealt with. These words can be incorporated in the class chart. Children may extend their reading to include stories and poems about birds.

Independent Writing

Children can now write their own simple report on birds. They will be able to use the overall structure suggested in the modelled and shared writing session. Their independent reading will prove to be a rich source of information. They will understand that the notes which they made can serve a practical purpose. They will be using words which they have talked about and investigated and will have extended their ability to apply a range of strategies when spelling.

Encourage children to carry out elementary proof reading. Discuss the importance of legible handwriting and sufficient spacing to assist readers to recognise misspellings.

At another time children might enjoy writing poems about birds. This would help them to think about the difference between words that are used for creative writing and reports.

Sharing and Reflecting

Children will have many discoveries to share. Their Spelling Journals will be full of new words and different ways of representing sounds. (see *Spelling: Resource Book* Chapter 2).

Help children to think about relationships between words, their roots, derivatives and structures, by drawing different representations, such as a network, a chain, an explosion chart. Introduce these slowly over time, using contexts which make sense to children.

Children need to be guided to talk about the processes they have used, such as how they found the derivation of a word, or how they identified key words which would help them in their writing. Don't forget to use the children's class spelling chart (see page 71).

Integrated and On-going Learning

The pathway described above demonstrates how the shared reading session and modelled writing sessions focus on a particular concept to prepare and equip children for a subsequent writing activity in which they can experiment with and apply the concept. During the day every opportunity is taken to support children's learning of the chosen concept in contexts which make sense to them through further modelled and independent writing, shared reading or complementary activities. At the end of the day children have an enhanced self-image and a strong sense of what they have learned and achieved as they have been able to pin down, share and report on their learning.

Context 1: Modelled and Shared Reading

Modelled and shared reading continue to provide contexts which help children extend their current understandings. The strategies readers use are made explicit. Features of words are discussed and interesting words noted for future reference. Children's' developing understandings will be reflected in their writing. Shared reading enables children to interact with print and with other readers in exciting, supportive and purposeful ways. Modelled reading gives them insights into the strategies readers use to create meaning.

Modelled and shared reading provide one of the most powerful contexts for productive teaching and learning about the way that written language works, the processes readers use and the strategies writers employ.

Teaching Suggestions

- All the subject areas will provide rich sources of informational texts. It is a good idea to introduce new concepts and unfamiliar words in a shared reading session, when children can learn how to use what they know about the structure and content of the text to help them make informed guesses or reasonable predictions about the meanings of words or phrases. This is an excellent context in which to demonstrate to children the links between meaning and spelling.
- Newspapers sometimes have sections for schools which might be too difficult for individuals but can be used for shared reading. Advertisements often feature mis-spellings or alternative representations of words which can trigger discussion, e.g. 'Steak 4 Sale'.
- The reading of poetry can be modelled by the teacher. This can be the prelude to choral or individual reading. This type of activity can help children develop a sense of the rhythm of language.
- A story can be serialised and read each day.

Challenge children to:

- focus on factors such as prefixes, suffixes, consonant digraphs. Collect examples from the text and chart them.
- underline the parts of words which rhyme and note whether or not the letter patterns are the same.
- classify words according to a specific letter pattern and then classify them according to the sounds represented, e.g. practise/promise; wise/advise/rise
- examine the function of words in a sentence. For instance, they can cover a 'doing word' and replace it with another word. At another time children can cover a noun or an adjective.
- change a story from the present to the past tense or vice versa. Ask them to discover what happens to the verbs. They can make a list of the verbs in the present and past tenses and construct rules which they can test and apply in other contexts.
- make a list of all the words in a text which have double letters. Try and uncover any common factors.
- collect singular nouns and make them plural. Collect plurals and make them singular. Group like words together, e.g. those in which an s is added - cat/cats; those in which es is added - box/boxes; those in which y is replaced with ies - story/stories; those which don't change - sheep/sheep.

Teaching Emphases

Use modelled and shared reading sessions to expose children to:
- the joy of reading
- sharing written language discoveries with others
- new vocabulary appropriate to different text types
- high interest and high frequency words from familiar texts
- Critical features of words
    - letter patterns
    - common English letter sequences
    - little words in big words
    - word roots
    - prefixes and suffixes
- Sounds and words
    - rhyme, rhythm and repetition
    - onomatopoeia
    - the segmentation of words into syllables
    - the segmentation of words into a sequential series of sounds
- Sounds and symbols
    - that letter names are constant but the sounds they represent will vary
    - that a letter or combination of letters may represent a range of sounds
    - that the same sound can be represented by different letters or letter combinations.

Context 2: Complementary Activities

Teaching Suggestions

- Involve children in word sorting and categorising activities (see *Spelling: Resource Book*), using:
  - meaning
  - letter patterns
  - sound
- Challenge children to
  - find words within words, e.g. teacher - each, ache, her, he, tea, teach
  - collect words with the same letter pattern in them, e.g. the -there, then, their, other, mother, father, brother and one - gone, done, bone, alone, none, phone
  - collect homonyms, e.g. wind, park, light, fly (*Spelling: Resource Book*)
  - make a list of homophones, e.g. two/too, hear/here
- Play
  - What Comes Next? (see *Spelling: Resource Book* Chapter 4)
  - word building games, e.g. in, win, wind, windy
  - Snap and Fish, matching words with the same letter patterns or sounds
  - games focused on blends, such as matching blends with word endings in Bingo or spinning wheel games
- Use mnemonics and encourage children to invent some, e.g.
  - My pal is the principal
  - Friend to the end
  - All the Es are in the cemetery
  - A piece of pie
- Create contexts in which children can invent or solve secret messages - see *Spelling: Resource Book*.

Proof Reading

(See *Spelling: Resource Book*, Chapter 4)
At this phase of development it is important that children are aware of the need to proof read written work, both during writing and afterwards. These skills will have been modelled for children incidentally during modelled writing sessions. It is now important to undertake specific teaching in this area. The following strategy is suggested:

- Take a piece of children's writing which has been written by a child in the Phonetic Phase of spelling development. It may be possible to procure an appropriate piece from a previous year, as it is important that the author of the writing is not known.
- Make an exact replica of the writing on a large piece of butcher's paper, or on an overhead transparency.

- Ask a small group or the whole class to help you proof read the writing.
- Read it through with the children before you start.
- Ask the children if they can find anything they would like to put right to make the writing easier to read.
- Accept any suggestions and act on them. For instance, a child might notice that there should be a gap between two words; another might notice that some letters are in upper case and some in lower case; spelling might be queried or a word might be seen to be missing.
- In each instance, ask the children to suggest what might be done. If they feel that a word is misspelled, encourage them to suggest or look for an alternative spelling. Model writing the word three different ways and decide which option looks right.
- Do not expect that all mistakes will be noticed or put right. When the children cease to offer suggestions, do not pursue the matter further.
- Recap the proofing suggestions, making sure that all are clearly marked or inserted on the paper.
- Take the working copy down and tell the children that you will re-write it incorporating their suggestions.
- Produce the edited copy in a subsequent session and discuss it with the children.

This proof-reading activity will soon become part of the regular routine of the classroom. If it can be seen as a privilege to have others help with the proofing of work, it may be possible to encourage children to volunteer their own work. This can be most productive if it can be managed in such a way that it enhances self-esteem.

Teaching Emphases

Complementary activities provide opportunities for children to refine and consolidate specific knowledge and understandings such as:

- understandings about words:
  - that a word can be segmented into syllables
  - that words may consist of a variety of parts such as roots, prefixes and suffixes
  - that rules can be discovered that govern the structure of words, such as making singular nouns plural or changing verbs into the past tense, etc. (see chapter on Word Study in *Spelling: Resource Book*)
  - that words fulfil a variety of functions in a sentence, such as 'doing' words, 'describing' words
  - that some words can be combined together to make another word
  - that words can rhyme with each other, but that rhyming words need not have identical letter patterns
- phonological awareness:
  - that a word can be segmented into a sequence of separate sounds
  - rhyme, rhythm and repetition
  - onomatopoeia
  - the concept of rhyming words
  - the segmentation of words into syllables
  - that a word can be segmented into a series of individual sounds
- critical features of words:
  - letter patterns
  - common English letter sequences
  - little words in big words
  - word roots
  - prefixes, suffixes
- sounds and symbols:
  - initial letter sounds
  - that letter names are constant, but the sounds they represent will vary
  - that a letter can represent a range of sounds
  - that the same combinations of letters can represent different sounds
  - that the same sound can be represented by different letter combinations.

Context 3: Modelled and Shared Writing

A wide range of different forms of writing are undertaken by the teacher and shared with the children. The teacher shows how successful writers meet challenges by 'thinking aloud', solving problems and making decisions. Children learn that writers change and adapt texts to suit themselves, their purpose and their audience. They learn how to manipulate words to serve a writer's purpose.

Teaching Suggestions

- Forms of writing which can be modelled or jointly constructed:
  - Letters
  - Addressing envelopes
  - Re-told stories
  - Created stories
  - Reports
  - Recounts
  - Comic strips
  - Memos
  - Lists
  - Labels for science/maths tables
  - Class diary
  - Limericks, haiku
  - Notes in different content areas
  - Summaries
  - Directions/instructions
  - Serial
  - 'Press releases' to advertise coming class or school events
  - Alphabet books
  - Wall stories
  - Captions for a mural
  - Class charts
  - Overhead projector transparencies
  - Chain writing - the teacher starts a sentence, breaks off after two words, hands the chalk to a child who writes the next two and so on
- When talking about words or letters in context encourage children to make connections with print they have encountered in other contexts
- Encourage children to substitute character names with their own names and place names with local names in poems or stories which are being retold.
- Continue to carry out oral cloze activities.
- Challenge children to create word chains or networks, which link words by association, before writing about a specific topic.

- Ask children to identify words from a text with the same sound. Accept all suggestions regardless of visual patterns. Record the words and then ask the children to group the words according to visual patterns.
- Develop activities from texts that are being written such as identifying and classifying all the letters which represent the same sound, e.g. girl, pearl, hurl, fern.
- Develop activities from texts which are being written such as identifying a letter pattern and discovering how many sounds it can represent, e.g. flood, good, zoo, book
- Construct a class dictionary from words in jointly constructed texts, emphasising alphabetical order.
- Ask children to select high frequency words from written texts to add to class word bank.
- Take every opportunity which arises to model editing and proof reading skills in context.

Teaching Emphases

Use modelled and shared writing sessions to expose children to spelling strategies such as:

- considering a word to see if it looks right
- writing a word down three times and deciding which attempt looks right
- thinking of common letter sequences
- identifying the critical features of a word
- using print around the room as easy references
- using a dictionary
- having-a-go and taking risks
- considering the components of words:
  - common letter patterns such as ea, ir, ou
  - short words within longer words
  - plural forms
  - word endings such as -ed, -ing
  - compound words
- considering sounds and symbols:
  - digraphs
  - blends
  - the same sound represented by different letters
  - the same letter sequence which represents different sounds
  - proof-reading strategies.

Context 4: Independent Reading

It is through independent reading that children are able to use their developing understandings about the structure and sounds of words to construct meaning. They need periods of time when they can explore books without stress, knowing that they can work things out secure in the knowledge that nobody is looking over their shoulders or asking them questions. It is important that all children are given the opportunity to enjoy books in the way that suits them best. It is often at these times that a great deal of consolidation and extension takes place.

Teaching Suggestions

- The reading corner provides a wide range of books, both fact and fiction, which are changed regularly. Magazines and comics offer readers a change of diet and a different sort of reading experience.
- Any theme or investigation which is taken up by the class will provide a springboard for reading of all types of text. A broad range of informational texts are available which are well structured and attractive to the reader.
- If project work is undertaken it should involve research which is genuine and interesting. Children will become increasingly familiar with the library and confident to access books to meet their needs.
- Each subject area provides opportunities for children to follow written instructions. Children will also become familiar with timetables, schedules and other factual guides.

Teaching Emphases

Children will use independent reading opportunities and subsequent discussion to further their knowledge about:
- language appropriate to different text types
- new vocabulary
- high interest and high frequency words from familiar texts
- common letter patterns
- words that they 'know' without 'having to think'.

Context 5: Independent Writing

Independent writing continues to provide one of the most powerful vehicles for applying, clarifying and further developing understandings and strategies essential to both reading and writing. It is when children are writing independently that teachers are able to observe what they do. Children's written products are windows into their minds, as they provide visible evidence of their current understandings. The more children write, the more they focus on print, and the ways in which they can use the written language for their own purposes. As they write they develop more effective strategies and construct deeper understandings about the writing process. Classrooms which encourage children to experiment and take risks, and which give them freedom to express themselves through the spoken and written word, provide contexts in which children achieve their potential as active and effective learners and competent spellers.

Teaching Suggestions

- Shared reading sessions will provide a springboard for a great deal of independent writing.
- Experiences at home and at school also provide motivation for writing.
- Subject-specific learning experiences engender a range of purposes and audiences for writing which will challenge children to produce different forms of writing.
- Class displays, such as the science table, will provide reasons for writing comments, labels and reports.
- A class mailbox can be used for the exchange of notes.
- Letters can be written for a range of purposes.
- A suggestion box can be set up with facilities for writing. Ensure that responses are made to all ideas.
- A notice board can be provided in the reading corner. Children can use it to make comments on books read or suggestions for books they would like to get hold of.
- A range of resources can be made available in the writing corner, such as picture dictionaries, dictionaries, a thesaurus and books of class word banks which have been jointly compiled and are now displaced by topical word banks.
- A wide variety of printed materials can be made available to the children. These can be used as a resource for children who are searching for new words on a topic or as a reference for children to return to if they wish.
- A spelling discovery board can be used by children to display their latest discoveries about words and spelling and to learn from the discoveries of others. It will provide a very useful springboard for discussion.
- A class alphabet book can be compiled into which children transfer words from their personal word banks.

- Current class word banks can be displayed which incorporate words from themes and subject areas. High frequency words can be included as can interesting or unusual words discovered by the children.
- Provide opportunities for children to write lists of requirements and procedures for art and craft, cooking, sport, maths activities, expeditions etc.
- Make individual language experience books for the reading corner. Use the necessity for writers to be aware of the needs of readers to teach and reinforce proof-reading and editing skills.
- Encourage pairs of children to write cooperatively, producing books for the reading corner.
- Encourage individuals or small groups to create retell books and books of text innovations.
- Encourage children to create cartoons with speech bubbles and write captions and titles for their work.

Teaching Emphases

These and many other writing contexts offer children opportunities to write for a wide range of purposes and audiences.

- Children use these opportunities to:
  - take risks
  - experiment with and apply concepts and strategies they have encountered in shared and modelled reading and writing
  - further develop their understandings about words, such as how words change their structure to meet different conditions, e.g. past tense, plural
  - further explore sound-symbol relationships
  - use high interest and high frequency words they have encountered in a range of contexts
  - experiment with the segmentation of spoken words into individual sounds and further develop their knowledge that a sound may be represented by a range of letter patterns and that a letter pattern may represent a range of sounds
  - apply syllabification strategies
  - undertake elementary proof reading
  - experiment with compound words and with the components of words.

Children learn through problem solving, they learn to write by writing and to spell as they represent words. When children are given opportunities to do so, they will apply and refine the understandings they are developing in shared and modelled reading and writing sessions.

Context 6: Sharing and Reflecting

In a busy classroom it is very easy to leave sharing and reflecting times until last and then find that there is no time for them.

Sometimes it seems as if quiet reflection on the processes and products of learning is a luxury rather than a necessity. Experience shows, however, that it is when children are given opportunities to step back from the immediate hustle of classroom life to think, talk and reflect, that their learning is consolidated and their confidence and belief in themselves is strengthened. Whatever slips away from an overcrowded schedule, it should not be these sessions.

Teaching Suggestions

- It is important that the teacher continues to model the process of reflecting and reporting on learning. Children will realise that there are two sorts of learning that they can talk about; the first is the facts they have learned, ('*What you have found out*'), e.g. the difference between *there* and *their*, or that *box* has an e before the s when it is plural; the second is the strategies they have learned, (*What you can do'*),e.g. write a word three times and choose the version which looks right, or that you only need to look at and learn the one or two letters you didn't get right rather than the whole word. When children are consciously aware of the range of strategies available to them, their control over writing and spelling is greatly enhanced. It may be helpful to have two separate sheets of paper on which to chart facts children know and strategies that they use. When children have become confident in differentiating between facts and strategies, they may wish to use this classification in their Learning Journals.

- Children relate well to pictorial representations. A useful way of assisting children to think about what they know is to draw different representations of knowledge, such as a network, a chain, an explosion chart etc. If these representations are introduced and modelled carefully and slowly over time, using contexts which make sense to children, they will start to use them spontaneously when illustrating an appropriate concept.

- It is important that all the discoveries relating to spelling continue to be written onto a large class chart. This will show children that their discoveries are important and that they can continue to supply missing features in the whole framework of spelling. The chart serves the additional purpose of providing an accurate record of what has been learned, so that steps can be taken to fill any gaps which might become evident (see illustration on page 71).

Teaching Emphases

Modelling of reflective thinking and reporting can include:
- feelings such as excitement, pleasure, apprehension
- a sense of achievement and pride
- knowledge of successful learning
- the value and importance of taking risks.

Strategies being learned are:
- categorisation and classification of words according to spelling patterns
- looking for visual patterns and common letter sequences in words
- identifying the most important parts of words
- finding letters or groups of letters that can represent different sounds depending on context or place in the word
- identifying sounds that can be represented by more than one letter or letters
- thinking about meaning as a strategy—particularly with inflected words
- continuing to develop word banks by incorporating theme, topic, high frequency and interesting words as they arise
- developing and using alphabetical lists
- proof-reading skills.

Phonetic Spelling Phase

A B C D E F G H I J K L M N O P Q R S T U V W X Y Z

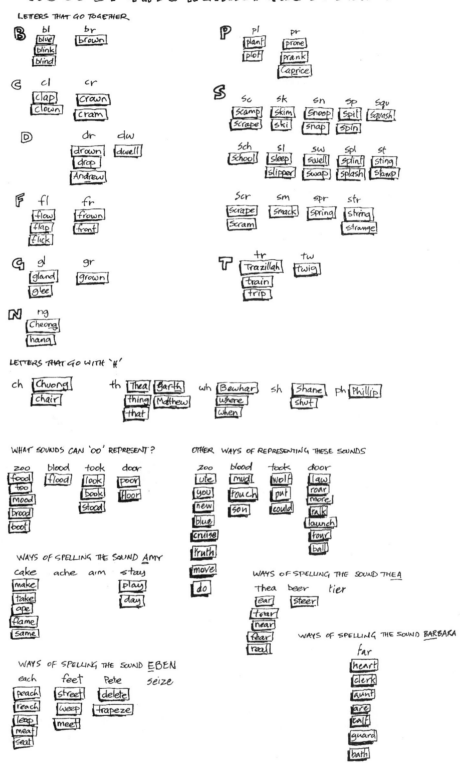

This chart would be gradually built up from the semi-phonetic chart (see page 52) as children discover new graphophonic relationships and letter patterns. The chart is constructed by the children, but written by the teacher, to ensure it can be easily read.

For Parents

How can I help my child with spelling?

- Continue to read to your child each day. Discuss interesting or funny words or words with unusual spellings.
- Make up mnemonics together to help with the spelling of difficult words, for instance, NIGHT—I'm Going Home Tonight, or, if having problems with a specific word ending such as 'ious'—I Owe U (you) Something
- Play increasingly sophisticated numberplate games in the car, for instance, trying to make a word which incorporates all the letters, or a nonsense phrase from the initial letters, such as HHC—Happy Hippos Croak.
- When your child writes or brings work home it is very important that you focus on what has been written, not on the spelling. If you do mention spelling, always focus on the words which have been spelled right, rather than on the mistakes. Talk about mistakes in terms of 'You had a jolly good try at spelling that word, didn't you?'. Always encourage risk-taking and having-a-go and show that you value all attempts.
- Encourage your child to try simple crossword puzzles and acrostics.
- Play simple word games such as 'Hang the Man'. If it is possible encourage relatives to give commercial word games for birthdays.
- Enjoy jokes and riddles with your child, especially those which play on words.
- Try and set up a desk or writing table in a well lit area. Have available a children's dictionary and thesaurus. Keep a good supply of note pads, scrap paper and attractive writing paper as well as an ample supply of pens and pencils.
- Encourage your child to make birthday cards, write thank-you letters, send post cards and the like.
- Help your child use the 'look, cover, write, check' method for learning words, concentrating on the part of the word he/she is not sure of rather than the whole word. Help the child divide the word into syllables.
- Encourage children to read through their work and underline any words they are not sure about. Don't do this for them, and don't draw attention to those they might have missed. Encourage them to think about the words they have identified and try alternative spellings, choosing the one which looks right. When you assist, help cooperatively rather than *telling* as an expert.

My Mum is overdue.

Peacock
It has eyes on its feathers. It spreads
its feathers out to attract the female.
Its colours are blue, green, pink and purple.
It has feet that have long bits on the end.
It has things on the end of its head.

On my birthday we had an ice-cream cake and for tea we had a pizza. Mum made the pizza and when we finished we got to have some chips and after everyone finished we had the ice-cream cake.

Transitional Spelling
(from sounds to structures)

In this phase writers are moving away from heavy reliance on the phonetic strategy towards the use of visual and meaning-based strategies. They may still have difficulty recognising if a word 'looks right', but should be able to proof their known bank of words. Writing will show evidence of an increasing bank of learned words. To help writers at this point it is better not to emphasise phonics. They are competently using phonetic strategies and now need to extend their repertoire to include alternative strategies. Emphasise strategies such as the identification of visual patterns, critical features and meaning.

At all phases of development students will be copying, recalling and inventing words. Students at this phase will copy the whole word rather than letters sequentially.

This is a critical phase in the development of spelling. It often takes writers a long time to move through it. It is very important that teachers monitor students' progress carefully so that they can be given as much support and explicit teaching as possible. If writers do not receive sufficient support they may not progress beyond this phase.

The Princy Adventure
Once upon a time there lived a handsome prince. His mother was dying and he had to find some fruit to cure her. In the kingdom there were no fruit trees, so he had to take a dangerous trip to the enchanted kingdom. There was a castle and the young prince rode in through the tall hard doorways and past the strong, hard doors he saw lots of little goblins dancing on the floor. Strangely enough all except one person who was a princess were all different colours.

> The Princy Adventure
> Once upon a time thier
> lived a hansom prince. his
> mother was dying and
> he had to find some fruit
> to qurer her. In the kingdom
> there were no fruit trees
> so he had to take a dangeros
> trip to the enchanted kingdom.

> In the enchanted kingdom
> there was a castel and
> the yong prince rode in
> throug the tall hard doorways
> and past the strong, hard
> doors and he saw lots
> of little goblins dancing
> on the floor. Strangly
> enough all except one person
> who was a princess wer all
> different colours P.T.O.

The writer:

◆ **uses letters to represent all vowel and consonant sounds in a word, placing vowels in every syllable, e.g. dangerous, enchanted, castel (castle)**
◆ **is beginning to use visual strategies, such as knowledge of common letter patterns and critical features of words, e.g. silent letters, double letters**
• uses visual knowledge of common English letter sequences when attempting to spell unknown words, e.g. dangerous, throug (through), enough, different, fruit
• uses vowel digraphs liberally, but may be unsure of correct usage, e.g. thier (there)
• syllabifies and correctly inserts a vowel before the 'r' at the end of a word, e.g. mother
• spells inflectional endings such as ...tion, ...ious, ...ight, ...ious conventionally
• includes all the correct letters but may sequence them incorrectly, e.g. castel (castle)
• usually represents all syllables when spelling a word, e.g. uncontrollabley (uncontrollably)
• is extending bank of known words that are used in writing, e.g. different, princess, dangerous, enough
• is beginning to use knowledge of word parts, e.g. prefixes, suffixes, compound words.

Transitional Spelling Indicators

The writer:

- ◆ **uses letters to represent all vowel and consonant sounds in a word, placing vowels in every syllable, e.g. holaday (holiday), gramous (grandma's), castel (castle), replyd (replied), gorrillas (gorillas)**
- ◆ **is beginning to use visual strategies, such as knowledge of common letter patterns and critical features of words, e.g. silent letters, double letters**

- uses visual knowledge of common English letter sequences when attempting to spell unknown words e.g. thousend (thousand), cort (caught), doller (dollar)
- uses vowel digraphs liberally, but may be unsure of correct usage, e.g. plaiied (played), kaingarows (kangaroos), ailyen (alien)
- may have over-generalised the use of silent 'e' as an alternative for spelling long vowel sounds, e.g. mite (might), biye (buy), chare (chair), moste (most), rane (rain), growe (grow), ocaye (okay)
- syllabifies and correctly inserts a vowel before the 'r' at the end of a word, e.g. 'brother' instead of 'brothr', 'water' instead of 'watr'
- spells inflectional endings such as …tion, …ious, …ight, …ious conventionally
- includes all the correct letters but may sequence them incorrectly, e.g. yuo (you), shose (shoes), Micheal (Michael), thier (their), recieve (receive)
- is beginning to make spelling generalisations, e.g. uses some double letters correctly
- is able to proof read known bank of words
- is beginning to use knowledge of word meanings, e.g. sign/signature, medicine/medical, circle/circular
- usually represents all syllables when spelling a word, e.g. uncontrollablely (uncontrollably)
- is extending bank of known words that are used in writing, including some subject specific words, e.g. February, Christmas, restaurant, diameter, conservation, scientific
- is beginning to use knowledge of word parts, e.g. prefixes, suffixes, compound words
- uses more difficult homonyms and homophones correctly, e.g. sore/soar, pour/poor, board/bored
- is willing to have-a-go at spelling specialised words found in specific subject areas such as science and social studies, e.g. experament (experiment), abatories (abattoirs), lattitude (latitude), electrisity (electricity)
- is aware of the importance of standard spelling for published work
- is willing to use a range of resources
- has an interest in words and enjoys using them.

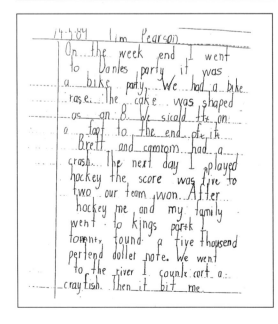

Teaching Notes

In the Transitional Phase writers move from a dependency on sound to developing awareness of structure. They begin to encounter and tackle challenges such as the rules of pluralisation; when to double letters and how to deal with affixes. They realise the complexity of the spelling system and set about gaining control over it. Writers usually stay in the transitional phase for a long time. They need to learn to use specific strategies such as the application of knowledge of meaning, morphology and visual patterns. Writers who do not come to terms with spelling strategies which take them beyond graphophonic relationships into the structural components of the language may never enter the independent phase of spelling.

The teaching emphasis continues to focus on classification of words through identifying common patterns. Children need to learn how to focus on the critical features of words. They need to develop strategies for remembering words, learning new words and locating the words they need and want to write.
Children in this phase also need the opportunity to focus on groups of words rather than words in isolation. This enables them to make generalisations about word patterns and to formulate rules.

Major Teaching Emphases

Transitional spellers need to develop familiarity with many common patterns of spelling through reading, writing and specific spelling activities.
They also need opportunities to focus on groups of words rather than words in isolation.
This enables them to make generalisations about word patterns and to formulate rules.

◆ **continue to emphasise visual patterns encouraging children to focus on patterns and to classify words**
◆ **focus on word meaning and word derivations as a guide to spelling, e.g. sign – signature**
◆ **teach strategies for remembering the correct spelling of difficult words**
◆ **teach strategies for spelling new words**
◆ **encourage writers to generate alternative spellings in order to select the right one**
◆ **encourage writers to hypothesise and generalise, e.g. rules for plurals and syllabification**
◆ **encourage the use of words not previously used to enlarge spelling vocabulary**
◆ **continue the development of word banks and class alphabetical lists**
◆ **continue to model and teach proof-reading skills**
• continue to explore sound-symbol relationships
• continue to focus on the critical features of words
• teach mnemonics to help remember difficult words
• discuss the social responsibility of spelling
• encourage children to think about spelling audience
• continue to provide a wide range of reading materials

At all phases:

◆ model writing in a variety of contexts
◆ encourage students to reflect on their spelling strategies
◆ encourage children to reflect on their understandings, gradually building a complete picture of the spelling system
◆ ensure that students have opportunities to write for a variety of audiences and purposes
◆ encourage students to take risks and have-a-go at spelling words they need to write.

◆ *Entries in bold are considered critical to the children's further development.*

Creating Effective Classroom Contexts

The following teaching sequence illustrates how strategies such as applying knowledge of common letter patterns and word derivations and using self-generated rules can be reinforced and consolidated in activities throughout the day (shared reading, complementary activities, independent reading, independent writing, shared writing, sharing and reflection). These activities also provide contexts in which concepts such as critical features of words and sound-symbol relationships can be further consolidated and extended. Positive attitudes to spelling and word study continue to develop as children experience success and enjoyment in their work. Activities are structured for individuals, small groups or the whole class, according to the children's needs and the demands of context and purpose and audience.

Shared Reading

Shared reading sessions could focus on the structure and content of fairy stories. It would be made clear to the children that they are going to explore the genre as competent readers and writers rather than as young children.

A wide variety of fairy stories can be read, including spoofs and those modern versions which operate in a 'back-to-front' fashion. Children can be encouraged to analyse the structure of the stories in such a way that they will recognise that the structure is based on sequences of three episodes, with three main characters, e.g. *The Three Bears* (who, of course, have three chairs, three bowls of porridge, three beds…), *The Three Little Pigs* (who build three houses…), *Aladdin*, who has three wishes, *The Three Billy Goats* Gruff, etc.

Complementary Activities

The triple structure of traditional fairytales can trigger an inquiry into the origin of the prefix 'tri'. Children can then investigate the use of bi…, quadr…, quin…, sext… Additional activities can be structured to focus around the use of prefixes and suffixes. Homophones and homonyms also provide a fascinating field for investigation.

Children's use of plurals can generate an investigation. Children need to control the construction of rules. Even if they do not get a rule quite right, or do not uncover the whole rule, their construction should be allowed to stand until they are constrained to adapt or change the rule.

The game 'What Comes Next' (see *Spelling: Resource Book* Chapter 4) can be played daily to reinforce knowledge of letter patterns such as ..ious, …tion, …ough. Older children may wish to introduce additional elements to make the game more complex, such as additional

points to children who identify the derivation of a word, or to children who identify a word with a foreign root.

Independent Reading

Children enjoy searching for fairy stories which fit the 'tri' structure. This provides an excellent opportunity for children to experience reading as objective researchers; standing back from the text and observing structure and content rather than becoming personally involved. They will notice words they have generated in brainstorming sessions and will further consolidate understandings about word structures that are developing. The question of gender stereotyping could well arise, and they may be interested to pursue an investigation into emotive and biased use of words.

Modelled and Shared Writing

The class might decide to write fairy stories for the Year One children. The first attempt could be a cooperative venture, focusing, for instance, on *The Three Wise Wombats of Wagin*. During the writing of the story the teacher could draw attention to common letter patterns and could model the technique of writing a word three times to see which version looks right. When the first draft is finished, encourage children to proof read their work. Proof-reading and editing skills are held in high esteem and can be shown to be essential if readers are to gain maximum benefit from the writing. A word-count activity could be introduced to help children monitor their proof-reading skills.

Independent or Paired Writing

Children will be eager to write their own stories. This is an occasion when writing with a partner could be a very productive exercise. The first session can be devoted to brainstorming ideas and drawing up a plan. In subsequent sessions ideas will be fleshed out and refined as the stories take shape. Critical reading, editing and proofing will assume great importance as the readers will be young and still struggling with concepts and conventions of print. Children will be praised for trying out their developing spelling strategies and for using their Have-a-go pads to experiment with letter patterns and sound-symbol relationships.

Sharing and Reflecting

Children are now more able to reflect on their own learning.

Learning Journals should be given very high status. A discussion might be held in which individuals share with others the different ways in which they represent what they have learned. It is important that each individual approach is valued and given due consideration and that there is no sense of one method being better than another.

Integrated and On-going Learning

If a concept or strategy is first introduced, then reinforced in shared reading and modelled writing sessions, children will confidently apply and develop it in their own writing. During the day every opportunity is taken to support children's learning of the chosen concept or strategy in incidental activities and through further modelled and independent writing. At the end of the day children are consciously aware of what they have learned and achieved as they have been able to reflect, share and report on their learning.

Context 1: Modelled and Shared Reading

Modelled and shared reading continue to provide contexts that help children extend and consolidate their current understandings. The first reading of any text is carried out to share overall meaning and interruptions to the reading are minimal. After this the text is used as a fertile field for investigation and analysis. A major focus is placed on critical reading strategies and understandings. The strategies readers use to make meaning are made explicit. An incidental focus may then be placed on words to enable children to gain insights into and control over features of words and how they are manipulated to make meaning. Children's developing understandings will be reflected in their writing. Shared reading enables children to interact with print and with other readers in exciting, supportive and purposeful ways. Modelled reading gives children insights into the strategies readers use to create meaning.

Modelled and shared reading provide one of the most powerful contexts for productive teaching and learning about the way that written language works, the processes readers use and the strategies writers employ.

Teaching Suggestions

- Continue to share texts of different types across all subject areas, for instance:
  - narratives (English, history)
  - recounts (English, Social Studies, Maths, Health, Science)
  - procedures (Social Studies, Maths, Health, Science, Art and Craft, Cooking)
  - reports (English, Social Studies, Health, Science)
  - expositions (English, Social Studies, Health, Science)
- Newspaper articles can be used for shared reading.
- The reading of poetry can be modelled by the teacher. This can be the prelude to choral or individual reading. It is often easier for children to appreciate and construct meaning from poetry if it is read to them first.
- A story can be serialised and read each day.
- Focus on factors such as prefixes, suffixes, compound words, consonant digraphs and blends. Encourage children to collect examples from a text, categorise and chart them.
- Challenge children to focus on the parts of words which rhyme and note whether or not the letter patterns are the same.
- Encourage children to classify words according to specific letter patterns. Identify the sounds represented. After this they can classify the words according to the sounds represented, e.g. trouser/pound/found; you/

wound; shoulder/boulder/mould; could/should/would; house/mouse; young; brought/sought.
- Ask children to problem-solve the function of words in a sentence. For instance, cover a verb, noun, adjective or adverb and ask children to replace it with another word. Encourage children to discover that all the words they suggest are words which fulfil the same function.
- Create a situation where children change a story from the present to the past tense or vice versa. Let them discover what happens to the verbs. They can make a list of verbs in the present and past tenses and construct rules which they can test and apply in other contexts.
- Continue to ask children to gather evidence regarding pluralisation, e.g. chair/chairs; kiss/kisses; fizz/fizzes; tomato/tomatoes; calf/calves; reef/reefs. Jointly construct rules which govern the process.
- Children can collect evidence from shared texts regarding double letters. For instance, after examining the evidence they might conclude that 'you double l, f or s after a single short vowel at the end of a word, e.g. tall, stiff, mess, fluff'. Are there any exceptions?
- Ask children to investigate what happens to *ay* at the end of a word when that word is extended, e.g. silly/silliness; carry/carriage; hurry/hurried. Are there any exceptions?

- Challenge children to discover what happens to a final consonant when a word is extended, e.g. plan/planned; begin/beginning. Are there any exceptions?
- New concepts and unfamiliar words can be introduced in shared reading sessions. The teacher can model strategies for accessing meaning through background knowledge, context and textual information. Children can be encouraged to make informed guesses or reasonable predictions about the meanings of words or phrases.

Teaching Emphases

Use modelled and shared reading sessions to expose children to:
- language appropriate to different text types
- new vocabulary
- high interest and high frequency words from familiar texts
- strategies readers use to make meaning from texts through word identification:
  - syntactic cues
  - semantic cues
  - visual patterns and common letter sequences
  - focusing on critical features of words
- word meanings and derivations, prefixes, suffixes and compound words
- strategies for generating hypotheses regarding word structures and modifications
- new and interesting words
- sounds of words
  - rhyme and rhythm
  - onomatopoeia
  - alliteration
  - the segmentation of words into syllables.

Context 2: Complementary Activities

Teaching Suggestions

- Identifying Morphemic Relationships Between Words
  Teaching children to use morphemic knowledge will help them recall spelling.
  When planning activities select words from the children's own writing, class word banks, shared books, different curriculum areas and current themes, encourage children to:

  - collect compound words from personal writing, books, magazines and dictionaries

  - read through familiar stories to find works with particular endings, e.g. ed, ing, er, est. Children can add these words to class charts or personal lists

  - sort words to identify those with the same visual, sound or morphemic letter pattern

  - make compound words, e.g. by joining a word from column 1 to a word from column 2.

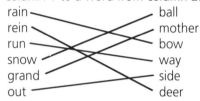

    rain — ball
    rein — mother
    run — bow
    snow — way
    grand — side
    out — deer

  - play 'Pairs' with compound words. Make sets of word which can be combined with other words to make a compound word, e.g. stair/case, foot/ball, fire/place

    Place cards face down. Children take it in turns to turn two cards over to try and find a pair. If they make a compound word they keep it and have another turn

  - make as many words as possible from a base word, e.g. soft, softer, softest, softly. Children can use these words to make up poems, songs, riddles and tongue twisters

  - use a dictionary to find words built from a particular morpheme, e.g.

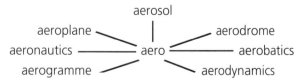

    aerosol
    aeroplane — aerodrome
    aeronautics — aero — aerobatics
    aerogramme — aerodynamics

  - develop lists of words based on well known derivations, e.g. aqua, aquatic, aqueduct

  - identify groups of words with related meanings, e.g. two, twin, twice, twenty; sign, signature, signal

  - investigate groups of words to identify base words

  - examine lists of words and their plurals, and discuss rules that govern these word changes.

- Using Mnemonics as a Memory Aid
  Introduce the children to the idea of using a memory aid or mnemonic to help remember some words. Encourage children to make up their own mnemonics. Help children to:

  - use creative phrases and sentences to help remember a word, e.g.
    'You 'fri' the 'end' of your 'friend'
    Take a bus into your business
    The Principal is my pal
    See the lie in believe

  - associate a word that is difficult to remember with one that is more easily remembered, e.g. here/there propeller/speller

  - use the meanings of words to provide a clue for correct spelling, e.g. buoy—a buoy warns of **u**nderwater **o**bjects, fourth—the fourth number is four.

- Sound-Symbol Relationships
  Continue to explore sound-symbol relationships. Teaching can be directed towards encouraging children to form association groups for words, to classify words and generalise this information to new words as they encounter them. Challenge children to:

  - identify words with a particular sound and sort them into spelling patterns. Children make generalisations about particular patterns

  - search for words with the same spelling pattern even though they may be pronounced differently, e.g. *ou* touch, cousin, house, rough, shout, regroup— according to sound pattern

  - play 'Make a Family' game. Each group is given a 'word family' card. Each child takes turns to write a word that belongs to that sound-symbol family. The winner is the team with most correct words

  - Sort words according to patterns, sound patterns, visual patterns and meaning patterns, e.g.

Meaning Patterns	Sound Patterns	
sign - signature	train	high
win - won	strain	lie
use - abuse	main	type
two - twice	remain	aisle
Visual Patterns		
could gone		
country tone		

cousin   done
couple   honey

– match words with clues, e.g.

the most important	chain
the seeds of plants such as wheat and oats	main
links joined together	grain

– encourage children to create puzzles for each other, e.g.

manipulate common English letter patterns, e.g.
Instead of the first '*d*' in *dead*, write: l, *br, inst, r, h, m, pl, spr.*
Write '*al*' in front of *most, ways, ready, so, though.*
After '*wh*', write *ole, ose, o, om, oever*

– complete cloze exercises. Use samples of children's own writing or excerpts from familiar shared books. Children are required to insert letter clusters, e.g. On Sund___ Mary went f___ a ___im with Jane. ('ay' 'or' 'sw'). Use deletions to focus attention on particular sound-symbol relationships

– discuss invented words and standard and non-standard spelling. Children can use common English letter patterns to make up their own words. These words can be illustrated or used in a poem or story. Charles Dodson's 'Jaberwocky' provides an excellent introduction to this activity

– make smaller words from a larger word, i.e. group words according to visual patterns and sound patterns, e.g. hospital

visual patterns			sound patterns		
tap	hop	pit	spot	so	to
lap	top	hit	top	post	
sap	lop	sit	hop	host	
			soap		

– play 'Rhyme Relay'
Children work in teams of two.
The first player calls a word, e.g. 'dog'.
The child in the opposing team calls out a rhyming word, e.g. 'bog'.
The second player in the first team calls 'cog'.
The second player in the opposing team calls 'frog'.
The team which calls the last word scores a point.
The opposing team then calls a word and the same sequence is followed.

• Editing and Proof Reading
Editing and proof reading are seen to be very important and children are now able to approach these skills at a more sophisticated level. They will have been modelled incidentally during modelled writing sessions. It is important that children become increasingly aware of the need to present work which is correct and easy to read. The following strategy is suggested:

– Take a piece of children's writing which has been written by a child in the Transitional Phase of development. It may be possible to use work which has been offered for this purpose by a member of the class. If so, great care needs to be taken to make the author feel good about the work and about the author's skill as a writer. If this does not seem to be appropriate, procure a piece of writing from a previous year

– Make an exact replica of the writing on a large piece of butcher's paper, or on an overhead transparency

– Ask a small group or the whole class to help you proof read the writing

– Read it through with the children before you start

– Ask the children if they can find anything they would like to put right to make the writing easier to read

– Accept any suggestions and act on them. For instance, a child might notice that there is a need for additional punctuation; another might notice that a sentence would be easier to comprehend if it was made into two separate sentences; spelling might be queried or an alternative word suggested

In each instance, ask the children to suggest what might be done. If they feel that a word is misspelled, encourage them to suggest or look for an alternative spelling. Model writing the word three different ways and deciding which option looks right

– Do not expect that all mistakes will be noticed or put right. When the children cease to offer suggestions, do not pursue the matter further

– Recap the proofing suggestions, making sure that all are clearly marked or inserted on the paper

– Take the working copy down and tell the children that you will re-write it incorporating their suggestions

– Produce the edited copy in a subsequent session and discuss it with the children

This proof-reading activity will now have become part of the regular routine of the classroom. If it can be seen as a privilege to have people help with the proofing of work, it may be possible to encourage children to volunteer their own work. This can be most productive if it can be managed in such a way that it enhances self-esteem.

Teaching Emphases

Complementary activities provide opportunities for children to refine and consolidate their understandings of:

- morphemic relationships
- compound words
- prefixes and suffixes
- visual letter patterns
- word derivations
- rules for pluralisation
- using mnemonics as a memory aid
- sound-symbol relationships
- proof reading.

Context 3: Independent Reading

Children in this phase of development have often have markedly different personal tastes in reading. Some lose themselves in fiction, others much prefer to pour over informational texts. Children need times when they are deeply engaged in pursuing and constructing their own meaning, because it is at such times that much valuable learning takes place.

Teaching Suggestions

- The reading corner provides children with on-going opportunities for choice and diversity in reading. Favourite stories containing rhyme, rhythm and repetition provide security for reluctant readers and give them pleasure and confidence. New stories fascinate and challenge children. Informational texts provide a different fare which is much enjoyed by many and which meets the needs of enquiring minds. Joke books, riddles and amusing jingles can be shared and enjoyed. Poetry extends children's horizons and brings into sharp focus the use of words as tools for writers.
- Areas devoted to specific subjects can also provide a rich source of reading material. The maths corner can offer reports, instructions and diagrammatic information and representation. The science table can display annotations, accounts and reports.
- The library will be increasingly well used by the children. Some will gravitate towards the informational and others to the fiction shelves. It is important that children are able to exercise their personal choice. Do not comment if they select books that seem too hard for them, they will ask for help if they need it or may simply enjoy looking at the pictures.

Teaching Emphases

Children will use independent reading opportunities and subsequent discussion to extend their reading ability and deepen their understandings about:
- language appropriate to different text types
- new vocabulary
- high interest and high frequency words from familiar texts

Children enjoy:
- Reflecting on what they have learned and accomplished
- Sharing written language discoveries with others
- Exchanging opinions and reactions.

Context 4: Modelled and Shared Writing

A wide range of different forms of writing are undertaken by the teacher and shared with the children. Children understand that the form and content of writing is dictated by purpose and audience, and that it is necessary to write as a reader. They realise that a writer has a responsibility to readers to ensure that their work is easy to read and spelled correctly. This realisation reinforces the need for careful proof reading. The teacher shows how successful writers meet challenges by 'thinking aloud', solving problems and making decisions. Children learn that writers change and adapt texts as they write, and after they have written, to suit themselves, their purpose and their audience.

Teaching Suggestions

- Suggested forms of writing which can be modelled or jointly constructed
  - letters
  - addressing envelopes
  - re-told stories
  - original stories
  - poems
  - reports
  - recounts
  - comic strips
  - memos
  - class diary
  - limericks, haiku
  - notes in different content areas
  - summaries
  - directions/instructions
  - 'press releases' to advertise coming class or school events
  - wall stories
  - class charts
  - overhead projector transparencies
  - chain writing - the teacher starts a sentence, breaks off after two words, hands the chalk to a child who writes the next two and so on
- Encourage children to:
  - make connections with words and structures they have encountered in other contexts and texts
  - relate a word to others that share the same morpheme
  - isolate affixes from root words
  - construct rules from evidence collected and subject them to on-going revues
  - use knowledge of visual patterns to determine whether a word looks right.
- Continue to carry out oral cloze activities.

- Create word chains or networks, which link words by association, before writing about a specific topic.
- Identify words from a text with the same sound. Record the words and then group the words according to visual patterns.
- Develop activities from texts that are being written such as identifying and classifying letter patterns and then grouping them according to sound, e.g. touch/cousin/rough, house/mouse, shout.
- Develop activities from texts which are being written such as identifying a letter pattern and discovering how many sounds it can represent, e.g. *ei*: their, ceiling, rein, weird, forfeit.
- Construct a class dictionary from words in jointly constructed texts, emphasising alphabetical order, using first, second, third letters etc.
- Select more high frequency words from written texts to add to class word bank.
- Continue to extend the use of proof-reading strategies.

Teaching Emphases

Use modelled and shared writing sessions to expose children to:
- conventions of print
  - terminology such as signal words, linking words, key words, parts of speech
- spelling strategies
  - considering a word to see if it looks right
  - writing a word three times to see which attempt looks right
  - identifying common letter sequences
  - identifying the critical features of a word
  - using print around the room as an easy reference
  - using a dictionary
  - having-a-go and taking risks
  - segmenting words into syllables
  - considering affixes
  - considering the meaning and thinking about the root word and derivations
  - mnemonics for remembering the correct spelling of difficult words
  - asking someone
- word study
  - letter patterns such as ough, ought, iour, ious
  - short words within longer words
  - plural forms
  - word endings such as -ed, -ing
  - rules for plurals, doubling letters, extending words
  - word meanings and word origins
- proof reading
- sounds and symbols
  - digraphs
  - blends
  - the same sound represented by different letters or letter patterns
  - the same letter sequence which represents different sounds
  - the application of strategies.

Context 5: Independent Writing

Independent writing continues to provide one of the most powerful vehicles for applying, clarifying and further developing understandings and strategies essential to both reading and writing. It is when children are writing independently that teachers are able to observe what they do. Children's written products are windows into their minds, as they provide visible evidence of their current understandings. The more children write, the more they focus on print, and the ways in which they can use the written language for their own purposes. As they write they develop more effective strategies and construct deeper understandings about the writing process. Classrooms which encourage children to experiment and take risks and which give them freedom to express themselves through the spoken and written word provide contexts in which children achieve their potential as active and effective learners.

Teaching Suggestions

- Shared reading sessions provide a springboard for a great deal of independent writing.
- Poetry reading forms an important component of a language arts program and inspires many children to write for themselves.
- Experiences at home and at school provide motivation for writing
- Creative and imaginative writing provides opportunities for the exploration of vocabulary and unusual syntactic forms
- Subject specific learning experiences engenders different forms of writing and new words.
- Class displays provide reasons for writing comments, labels and reports. A mathematics display area can provide a context for highly focused writing. A science centre, containing a wide variety of materials for experimentation, can also include reference books, writing materials, ideas cards (for reading and writing), observation cards or pads and a word bank of useful and topical words. A music centre can offer percussion instruments, music, paper for musical notation, song books, tape recorder and tapes and a music journal for children to note reactions, ideas and musical discoveries.
- A class mailbox can be used for the exchange of notes
- Letters can be written for a range of purposes.
- Provide a suggestion box with facilities for writing. Ensure that responses are made to all ideas.
- A notice board or response book can be provided in the reading corner. Children can use it to make comments on books read or suggestions for books they would like to get hold of.
- A range of resources can be made available in the writing corner, such as dictionaries, a thesaurus and class word banks which have been jointly compiled.

- A wide variety of printed materials, class charts and word lists are available to the children. These can be used as resources for children who are searching for new words on a topic or as reference points for children to return to if they wish.
- A spelling discovery board can be used by children to display their latest discoveries about words and spelling and to learn from the discoveries of others. It provides a very useful springboard for discussion.
- Current class word banks can be displayed with words from themes and subject areas. High frequency words can be included as can interesting or unusual words discovered by the children.
- Help children implement proof-reading strategies such as reading backwards, reading line-by-line.
- Encourage children to check spelling with a peer or peer reference group.
- Implement activities and strategies outlined in the *Spelling: Resource Book*.
- Introduce Spelling Journals if these are not already in use (see *Spelling: Resource Book* Chapter 2)
- Encourage children to list 'Strategies I can use when I want to spell a word I don't know', e.g.
  - write it down 3 times on my have-a-go pad and see which spelling looks right
  - look it up in a dictionary
  - break it up into syllables and think of common letter patterns
  - find it in a word bank or class chart
  - sound it out
  - think of the meaning and the derivation
  - focus on the critical feature of the word
  - ask a friend.

Teaching Emphases

Children use these opportunities to:
- take risks, try things out
- experiment with and apply spelling concepts and strategies they have encountered in shared and modelled reading and writing
- further develop their understandings about words and the ways in which words can be modified and extended
- further explore sound-symbol relationships
- use high interest and high frequency words they have encountered in a range of contexts
- further develop their knowledge that a sound may be represented by a range of letter patterns
- further develop their understanding that a letter pattern can represent a range of sounds
- apply syllabification strategies
- apply strategies for remembering the correct spelling of difficult words
- hypothesise, generalise and apply rules for plurals, doubling letters, extending words
- use strategies such as generating alternative spellings in order to select the right one
- think about word meanings, e.g. sign - signature
- write as readers, realising the importance of editing and proof reading.

Children learn through problem solving, they learn to write by writing and to spell as they represent words. When children are given opportunities to do so, they will apply and refine the understandings they are developing in shared and modelled reading and writing sessions.

Context 6: Sharing and Reflecting

It is extremely important that children continue to be given regular and frequent opportunities to stand back and reflect on their learning. They need to identify and talk about their achievements and the strategies they are developing. By now, children need fewer concrete aids to help them, such as puppets, but may still need prompts and scaffolds to guide their reflection.

Teaching Suggestions

- Continue to model the process of reflecting and reporting on learning, helping children to differentiate between *strategies*, such as the application of knowledge of meaning, root words, affixes and compound words in spelling, and *knowledge*, such as the meaning of palindrome, homophone or homonym. Children may wish to comment on or add to the knowledge items and try out the strategies suggested by their peers.

- When children are confident in differentiating between knowledge and strategies, they may wish to use this classification in their learning or spelling journals when recording what they have learned during the day or week.

- It is invariably helpful to represent knowledge in a variety of ways. The use of networks, branching tree structures, chains, pyramids and explosion charts of one type or another can be illuminating for children. If these representations are introduced and modelled carefully and slowly over time, using contexts which make sense to children, they will use them spontaneously when illustrating an appropriate concept, or making connections between words and ideas.

- It is important that a large class chart be used in conjunction with reflection sessions so that children's growing understandings can be carefully recorded as they are discussed (see illustration on page 91). Children need to be aware not only of their specific discoveries, but also how these discoveries fit into the big framework of the English spelling system. The chart provides a context which shows links, relationships and exemplars. At this stage it may well have become impossible to show everything on the same chart. If separate charts are made to accommodate different aspects of the spelling system, it is important that the links between these are made clear to the children. The chart(s) serve the triple functions of acknowledgment of learning, demonstration of systematic relationships and accurate record keeping.

Teaching Emphases

Children may identify achievements through:
- using visual patterns to classify words
- newly discovered sound-symbol relationships
- trying out alternative spellings in order to select the right one
- focusing on the critical features of words
- placing a focus on word meaning and derivations as a guide to spelling
- enjoying creating mnemonics as an aid for remembering difficult words
- constructing rules for plurals and syllabification
- using new words to enlarge spelling vocabulary
- understanding that good spelling makes it easier for other people to read writing
- using proof-reading skills.

Transitional Spelling Phase

ABCDEFGHIJKLMNOPQRSTUVWXYZ

CONSONANTS: BCDFGHJKLMNPQRSTVWXYZ

VOWELS: A E I O U

CONSONANT CLUSTER: bl, cl, fl, gl, sl   dw, tw
br, cr, dr, fr, gr, pr, tr
sc, sch, scr, sk, sm, sn, sw, sp, spl, spr, st, str.

Digraphs: ch, ph, sh, th, wh

Silent Letters: mn, gn, gh, ps, kn, mb

Short vowels: bat, bet, bit, bottle, but

Long Vowels:
a-e, ay, ai, eigh
plate pay plaid eight
e-e, ee, ea, y, ey
delete feet bead funny money
i-e, ie, igh, y, ye
bite die high my dye
o-e, oa, ow
bone moan blow
u-e, ew, ue oo
flute flew blue balloon

Other Sounds:
oy, oi, ow, ou, ir, er, ur
boy coin now bout stir term burn
or aw au oo all alk aigh
torn awful audience door tall stalk

Derivatives:
Parlour from French parler (speak)
delicatessen from Italian delicatezza

Pre-fixes: un- Pre- re- uni- bi- tri- quad- de-

Suffixes: -ive -ed -ness -full -tion

Compound words: grandstand football outcast breakfast

Root words: aqua – Latin – water; deka – Greek – ten; decima – Latin – tenth.

In this phase students are able to use a more decontextualised chart for reference purposes. The chart was originally constructed from the student's own contributions (see Phonetic Spelling Chart, p. 71). Students continue to make their own contribution to the chart.

For Parents

How can I help my child with spelling?

- Continue to read to your child regularly, discussing the way the author has used words and any interesting features of words that you notice.
- Do crossword puzzles together and play word games whenever you can.
- Ensure that your child reads a wide range of books, magazines, TV guides, recipes and instructions for making or operating things. Make good use of the library to extend the range of stories and informational books your child can read.
- Continue to keep a writing area well supplied with attractive paper and pens. Encourage your child to make birthday and Christmas cards and write letters, card etc.
- Encourage your child to keep a journal. This may be specially useful when on holiday or travelling. Respect her/his privacy.
- Always be interested in work your child brings home and ensure that you focus on what is being said rather than on spelling. If spelling is mentioned praise him/her for having-a-go and making a good approximation, rather than commenting on errors.
- When children are trying to learn a word:
  - first let them have-a-go at spelling it.
  - then note all the letters which are correct.
  - if some are incorrect, it will probably be for a good reason, for instance, a child might spell 'handsome' *hansom*. If this happens, praise the child for having a sensible go and spelling the word as she/he thinks it sounds.
  - then divide the word into the syllables *hand* and *some*, both of which the child will be able to spell. This will bring much better results than simply gazing at the word in an attempt to learn it.
  - if, on the other hand, the child has reversed letters, for instance *peice* instead of *piece*, help the child to focus only on the letters that are reversed rather than the whole word. 'Piece has ie in the middle, like pie'.
  - now employ the 'look, cover, write, check' method.
- If your child is having problems with spelling, two things may help:
  - providing encouragement by counting the words that are *right*, instead of the words that are wrong.
  - Learning one or two words well, rather than failing to learn ten or twenty. Talk this through with the teacher, who will know what is best for your child.

INVADERS SPACE ALIENS

Mars 4000 A.D. Saturday
Space aliens have attacked people living on the moon. The people living on the moon said 'We must destroy the space aliens before they destroy our planet.' At the moment the main colony is full of frightened people. The earth has sent someone to help the people living on the moon to help fight the space aliens.

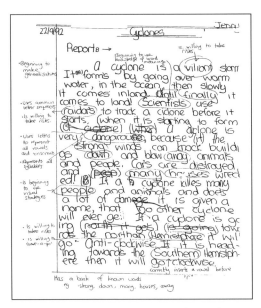

Cyclones Report

A cyclone is a violent storm. It forms by going over warm water in the ocean, then slowly it comes inland until finally it comes to land! Scientists use radar to track a cyclone before it starts.
A cyclone is very dangerous, because the strong winds can knock buildings down and blow away animals and people. Cars are destroyed and many houses wrecked. If a cyclone kills many people and animals and does a lot of damage it is given a name that no other cyclone will ever get. If a cyclone is going towards the northern hemisphere it will go anti-clockwise. If it is heading towards the southern hemisphere, then it will go clockwise.

Independent Spelling

In this phase children have become aware of the many patterns and rules that are characteristic of the English spelling system. When spelling a new word they use a multi-strategy approach. They have the ability to recognise when a word doesn't look right and to think of alternative spellings. Spellers in this phase will have accumulated a large bank of known words that they can automatically recall. Independent spellers are prepared to attempt unknown words by making use of prior knowledge to predict the most likely spelling. They view spelling as a problem-solving task. They want to use appropriate spelling and are prepared to proof read their writing.

At all phases of development children will be copying, recalling and inventing words. Independent spellers continue to use personal constructions when spelling unfamiliar words in draft writing.

(A monkey called Muffles has escaped from the circus.)
The first house he came to he ran joyfully out of, over the perfect flowerbed of soft blooms. He looked at the squashed rosebuds with delight. Muffles seized a handful and threw them at the prim lady trotting down the street. 'A - a - a - a - a - h, you wicked scallywag', she cried, and she lifted him swiftly and gave him a sharp tap on the backside … (He went inside a house to explore.) Muffles found it great fun to squirt toothpaste to the ceiling and when he looked in the mirror he saw an ugly face looking back at him. He was furious and threw the slippery soap at it, but it just bounced off … Once in the bedroom, Muffles wanted to look like the prim lady he had seen, so he grabbed the lipstick and smeared it on his face, (and over a lot of other things too), dress draped around his shoulders, a hat upside-down perched precariously on his head, and blush on his nose.

The writer:

◆ **is aware of the many patterns and rules that are characteristic of the English spelling system, e.g. common English letter patterns, relationship between meaning and spelling, e.g. fury, furious**

◆ **makes generalisations and is able to apply them to new situations, e.g. rules for adding suffixes, selection of appropriate letter patterns (-ion), e.g. handful, joyfully, slip - slippery, grab - grabbed**

◆ **accurately spells prefixes, suffixes, contractions, compound words**

◆ **uses context to distinguish homonyms and homophones, e.g. threw**

◆ **uses silent letters and double consonants correctly, e.g. immediately, bedraggled, trotting, grabbed**

◆ **effectively spells words with uncommon spelling patterns and words with irregular spelling, e.g. seized, pleasure, ceiling**

◆ **uses less common letter patterns correctly, e.g. seized, ceiling, precariously**

◆ **uses a multi-strategy approach to spelling (visual patterns, sound patterns, meaning)**

◆ **is able to recognise if a word doesn't look right and to think of alternative spellings, e.g. busted/burst**

◆ **uses syllabification when spelling new words, e.g. precariously**

◆ **has accumulated a large bank of known sight words and is using more sophisticated language.**

Independent Spelling Indicators

The writer:

◆ is aware of the many patterns and rules that are characteristic of the English spelling system, e.g. common English letter patterns, relationship between meaning and spelling

◆ makes generalisations and is able to apply them to new situations, e.g. rules for adding suffixes, selection of appropriate letter patterns (-ion)

◆ accurately spells prefixes, suffixes, contractions, compound words

◆ uses context to distinguish homonyms and homophones

◆ uses silent letters and double consonants correctly

◆ effectively spells words with uncommon spelling patterns and words with irregular spelling, e.g. aisle, quay, liaise

◆ uses less common letter patterns correctly, e.g. weird, forfeit, cough, reign

◆ uses a multi-strategy approach to spelling (visual patterns, sound patterns, meaning)

◆ is able to recognise if a word doesn't look right and to think of alternative spellings

◆ analyses and checks work, editing writing and correcting spelling

◆ recognises word origins and uses this information to make meaningful associations between words

◆ continues to experiment when writing new words

◆ uses spelling references such as dictionaries, thesauruses and resource books appropriately

◆ uses syllabification when spelling new words

◆ has accumulated a large bank of known sight words and is using more sophisticated language

◆ shows increased interest in the similarities, differences, relationships and origins of words

◆ is willing to take risks and responsibilities and is aware of a writer's obligations to readers in the area of spelling

◆ has a positive attitude towards self as a speller

◆ has an interest in words and enjoys using them

◆ is willing to use a range of resources and extend knowledge of words, including derivation, evolution and application.

Teaching Notes

A writer at this phase is aware of the many patterns and rules that are characteristic of the English spelling system. The writer is able to focus on relationships between words, make generalisations and apply them to new situations. The correct spelling of words or the identification of words is achieved mainly by visual familiarity. When spelling an unfamiliar word, however, the student will draw on a range of semantic, syntactic, morphological and phonological information.

Writing and reading activities will help to extend the writer's vocabulary and at the same time knowledge of the patterns of word structure based on graphophonic, morphemic and visual principles will be extended, refined and integrated.

Teachers should plan language activities across the curriculum that provide students with the opportunity to explore the ways words can be combined, extended and changed to suit the meanings required by writers in every situation. Students should be encouraged to accept responsibility for increasing spelling vocabulary.

Major Teaching Emphases

Independent spellers should be encouraged to accept responsibility for extending their spelling vocabulary. They should proof read all their written work as they are now able to spell most commonly used words correctly.

- ◆ **focus on meaning as a guide to spelling**
- ◆ **continue to explore derivations of words—meanings of foreign words as a guide to spelling**
- ◆ **consolidate and extend proof-reading skills**
- ◆ **continue to build up a systematic picture of the whole spelling system**
- ◆ **teach writers to use context as a guide to spelling**
- ◆ **reinforce strategies for remembering correct spelling of difficult words**
- ◆ **emphasise social importance of spelling—insist on correct spelling for public audiences, parents, other classes or principal**
- • continue to encourage approximations of new words
- • encourage writers to decide whether a word looks right
- • continue to build up a systematic picture of whole spelling system
- • encourage the use of words not previously used to enlarge spelling vocabulary
- • continue to develop dictionary skills by providing a wide range of dictionaries
- • continue to model the use of appropriate spelling strategies across a wide range of contexts
- • continue to provide a wide range of reading materials

At all phases:

- ◆ **model writing in a variety of contexts**
- ◆ **encourage students to reflect on their spelling strategies**
- ◆ **encourage children to reflect on their understandings, gradually building a complete picture of the spelling system**
- ◆ **ensure that students have opportunities to write for a variety of audiences and purposes**
- ◆ **encourage students to take risks and have-a-go at spelling words they need to write.**

◆ *Entries in bold are considered critical to the children's further development.*

Creating Effective Classroom Contexts

The following teaching sequence illustrates how strategies such as the exploration of meaning through previous knowledge, word derivations and contextual understandings can be reinforced, extended and consolidated in activities throughout the day. At this phase students take responsibility for their writing and understand that correct spelling enhances communication by facilitating reading. Activities are structured for individuals, small groups or the whole class, according to the children's needs and the demands of context and purpose and audience.

Shared Reading

A newspaper article could provide the focus for discussion and investigation, e.g. on the effects of tourism on the environment. The first and last paragraphs could be skimmed to obtain the flavour of the article. Participants could then hypothesise about issues, arguments and relevant words which are likely to emerge from the article. During the reading of the article, students could be encouraged to note key words and concepts. Arguments could be framed together with supporting evidence. In this context a list of words could emerge which present difficulties. Students can suggest possible meanings and can explain the reasons for their answers.

Independent Reading

Everyone will undertake to read as many related texts as possible. If there are a great many articles, small groups will choose an aspect of the topic which is of special interest and will read material which relates specifically to that aspect. Each group will identify and extract important information, provide a summary of the text and draw conclusions, make judgements and generalisations.

Shared Writing

The class will come together after sufficient time has been given for independent reading. Each group will report on its area of study. Common threads will be drawn out and listed. Areas of conflict will also be noted. Together a summary of findings will be first structured and then written for publication in the school magazine.

Complementary Activities

As a result of their reading, students may construct:

    skeleton outlines
    pyramids
    semantic grids
    flow charts
    retrieval charts.

An in-depth investigation of interesting or unfamiliar words can be undertaken. The roots and derivations of the words can form the basis of an exploration into their histories and devolution. Explosion charts can capture other words that have been generated as a result of discussion. Critical features of words, unusual patterns and changing meanings can be noted.

Independent Writing

A study of the environmental impact of tourism could lead students into writing for a range of purposes and audiences.

Letters could be sent to one of the two research centres which have been set up to study this topic. They are: Griffith University's International Centre for Eco-tourism Research and the World Travel, and Tourism Environment Research Centre, Oxford University, United Kingdom. Other letters could be written to local tourist organisations or conservation bodies. Reports could be written which would present findings to local government or community newspapers. Narrative and poetic writing could centre around emotive issues. Ensure that students proof read their work.

Sharing and Reflecting

The general issues and arguments raised will engender a great deal of reflective thought. Apart from these deeper issues, matters relating to the extension of vocabulary, the devolution of words and the emotional connotations of many of the words will emerge. The study of words will take on wider implications than before.

Integrated and On-going Learning

In this phase activities often emerge spontaneously from a general context, for instance, students who have been engaged in library research may wish to share an interesting text with others, so that a shared reading session takes place. The class may have chosen to focus on a specific aspect of writing, such as the use of metaphor, and this may lead to sharing which emerges from independent reading, or exploratory writing. The daily routines enjoyed by younger children are superseded. Students are able to integrate their thinking and transfer their learning across subject areas. Reflection and sharing times serve to pull the threads together so that each can benefit from the insights of the others.

Context 1: Modelled and Shared Reading

There is always a place for listening to stories. Adults derive as much pleasure from listening to a story as do children; the pity is that they seldom have the opportunity to indulge in this important activity. In upper primary classes and in secondary school, students should be exposed to literature of all sorts, in a context that is supportive, relaxing and enjoyable.

Teaching Suggestions

- It is often easier to appreciate poetry when it is heard rather than read. The rhythm and flow of the language and the meanings which lie below the surface are sometimes easier to access when the reading is the responsibility of another. Each individual is then able to revisit the poem and create personal meanings.
- Individual study occupies an increasingly large place in the lives of students as they move through the school. Techniques for dealing with an increasingly complex and specialised vocabulary can continue to be modelled in shared readings of subject-specific texts.
- Shared reading can provide a context in which the merits and demerits of opposing texts can be discussed. Bias can be detected and analysed. Stereotypes can be matched with reality and with the perceptions of readers who themselves come from diverse cultures and communities. Actual words used to produce effect can be identified. New and interesting words can be noted and word derivations and histories pursued.

Teaching Emphases

Students will use shared reading opportunities to extend and enhance their reading strategies and understandings about:
- a writer's manipulation of words to create an effect
- the structure of words
- word derivations and the evolution of meaning
- language appropriate to different text types
- new and challenging vocabulary
- high interest and high frequency words from familiar texts

Students enjoy:
- reflecting on what they have learned and accomplished
- investigating and analysing written language with others
- exchanging opinions and reactions.

Context 2: Independent Reading

Independent reading occupies an increasingly important place in the lives of students as they mature. They become less and less dependent on the direction given by their teachers and more inclined to explore new worlds. It is prolific readers who acquire an extensive vocabulary and who are confident to experiment with and explore words for themselves.

Teaching Suggestions

- A great deal of independent reading will be generated from studies of content across the subject areas. This will include a wide range of text types and forms of writing within the types.
- Independent research will assume a much greater focus for students. This will give them an opportunity to refine skimming and scanning skills and the use of strategies such as the identification of key words.
- The reading of fiction will also increase in importance as students interact with classical literature, modern novels and a wide range of forms including humour, satire and mystery.
- Students will read biographies, autobiographies and journals.
- Poetry will also be highly valued.
- Technical reading, instructions, maps and the like will be used in context.

Teaching Emphases

Students will use independent reading opportunities and subsequent discussion to extend and deepen their knowledge and awareness of:
- the possibility of multiple interpretations of a text
- the importance of challenging and questioning a text
- a wide range of different text types and of forms of writing within text types
- reading for different purposes
- language appropriate to specific text types
- words, their structure and use.

Context 3: Complementary Activities

Even when writers have gained mastery over the spelling system and, more importantly, learned what to do when they cannot immediately spell a word, there is still a need to structure relevant activities that enable them to come to grips with specific aspects of spelling.

Teaching Suggestions

Students continue to use word meanings as a guide to spelling words. English words that are connected in meaning have a common visual pattern, e.g. medic, medical, medicine. This knowledge of the meaning function of words can help students go straight to the meaning of written texts.

Encourage the exploration of the derivation of words as an activity which is challenging and fun. Whenever students come across new words, encourage them to look at the structure of the words and relate this to word meaning. Challenge children to:

- form other words from a root word using prefixes and suffixes, e.g. port - transport, report, support, portable, important
- select words from reading and writing, grouping words together that are related by meaning
- examine groups of words and identify the root word from which they are derived.
- use Latin or Greek roots to create an imaginary animal or plant, e.g. *mono-cornis-cephalus*, one-horn-head
- use old dictionaries to investigate the derivatives of words
- become involved in activities that focus on the meaning relationships between words, e.g. words with silent letters - signature/sign, nest/nestle
- identify base words from given lists of words, e.g. disinterested, uninterested, interested, interests
- use Latin and Greek roots to find the meanings of words
- identify words formed from two or more words, e.g. cap in the hand: handicap; motor - hotel: motel; breakfast - lunch: brunch
- identify and explore acronyms (words formed from initial letters of other words), e.g. laser - light amplification by stimulated emission of radiation
  - NASA - National Aeronautics and Space Administration
  - QANTAS - Queensland and Northern Territory Aerial Services
  - radar - ratio detection and ranging
  - scuba -self contained underwater breathing apparatus
  - ANZAC - Australian and New Zealand Army Corps

  - UNESCO - United Nations Educational Scientific and Cultural Organisation
- identify and discuss abbreviated words, e.g. refrigerator: fridge, budgerigar: budgie, telephone: phone
- identify and discuss portmanteau words (words which have been put together to form new words) e.g. from twist and whirl: twirl; from smoke and fog: smog; from flutter and hurry: flurry; from clap and crash: clash; from flame and glare: flare; from horrible and tremendous: horrendous
- identify onomatopoeic words (words which have been created to resemble sound), e.g. creak, boom, hiss, bang, buzz, whoosh, miaow, screech, tick, cackle, chant, chatter.
  These can be used in stories and poems. They can also be used for word hunts, e.g. find and list things that tick or hiss.
- search through texts for compound words
- select a piece of text from a book they are reading or a piece they have written and list all the words with prefixes/suffixes
- examine and classify words according to their countries of origin, e.g.

Germany	France	Japan
blitz	souffle	origami
kindergarten	restaurant	geisha
hamburger	boutique	kimono

- carry out open and closed word sorts (see *Spelling: Resource Book* Chapter 4).
- enter words on to a map of the world showing the countries of origin, e.g.
  - France - restaurant, boutique, discotheque
  - North America - squaw, wigwam, moccasin
  - Germany - hamburger, frankfurter, kindergarten
  - Japan - origami, haiku, bonsai
  - Australia - swagman, jumbuck, outback, humpy
  - Words from Aboriginal languages - corroboree, boomerang, kaditcha, yabber, yakker, dillybag
- identify words derived from people's names or titles, e.g.
  - cardigan - after Lord Cardigan
  - braille - named after Louis Braille
  - pasteurisation - after Louis Pasteur

– pavlova - after Anna Pavlova
– sandwich - named after the Earl of Sandwich
- use an encyclopedia to discover how the person's name came to be used for something, e.g. silhouette, Bunsen burner, galvanised iron, watt, volt, morse code
- examine Latin and Greek roots. Identify related English words. Students prepare charts showing relationships, e.g.
  'catastrophe' from Greek root 'cata'
  'education' from the Latin word 'educare'
  'contradict' from the Latin root ' contra'
  'measure' from the Greek root 'metron'
- sort words into the countries from which they originated, e.g. German, French, Spanish, Italian, Arabus, American, Indian, Hebrew, Greek. Use a dictionary to check, e.g.

dachshund	veranda
sauerkraut	tornado
kindergarten	volcano
bouquet	spaghetti
zucchini	alphabet
hurricane	algebra
tomahawk	assassin
cosmos	toboggan

- trace the root of a word, e.g. scribble from scribe - to write
- construct a branching tree structure, take any suggested word and brainstorm associations :

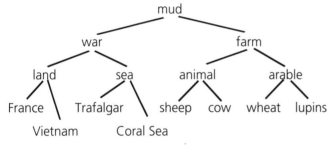

- brainstorm networks of words around a central focus, demonstrating the use of words for different purposes and across a range of contexts, e.g.

WATER

Poetic	Scientific	Agricultural	Domestic
ripple	hydraulic	irrigation	drain
life-giving	(ram/press)	hydroponics	washer
	H2O	dam	drink

- Instead of brainstorming words according to classification, encourage students to call out any word that comes into their heads after a key word has been called out. Write these down as they are called. Afterwards discuss the results and determine how they can be classified ,e.g.

HOUSE

Two-storey, brick, igloo, mobile, wood, stone, warmth, iron, palace, hen-house, home, apartment, holiday house, family, dog-house, wigwam, shelter, squatter, rent, cave, mortgage…
In this instance it might be decided to classify the words according to type, material construction, occupant, purpose, outcomes (benefits/disadvantages/ consequences)

- Metaphors and similes can be collected and charted. Students can then invent their own
- Students can also collect and research sayings that have their roots in history, such as:
  – four sheets before the wind
  – Aunt Sally
  – Davey Jones' locker
  – laughing stock
  – not worth a tinkers' curse
  – as mad as a hatter
  and sayings from other languages that have become part of our own, such as:
  – en suite
  – quid pro quo
  – in vitro
  – simpatico
  – post hoc
  – vice versa
  – agent provocateur.

Consulting an Authority

Continue to teach and systematically reinforce dictionary skills. A variety of different dictionaries should be available, so that the most appropriate can be selected for the purpose required, e.g. dictionary of synonyms, antonyms, idioms, thesaurus, etc. These can be used for any of the activities involving word searches.

It is sometimes assumed that writers at this phase of development will be able to use a dictionary competently and confidently. Many writers, however, need explicit instruction to help them move from their simple 'children's' dictionary to the adult version. Dictionary abbreviations and conventions need to be explained, as does the use of a root word in tracking down its derivatives.

Students can be challenged to:
- find all the meanings of a common word and write sentences to show the different meanings
- discuss different pronunciations of words which are spelled the same
  (encourage use of pronunciation key)
- choose interesting words from their reading and check the meanings in a dictionary
- locate the meanings of roots or prefixes in a dictionary
- engage in problem solving with meanings
  – What do these words have in common? fuchsia, camellia?
  – How could you use an ocarina?
  – How is organum like rosemary?

Proof Reading and Editing

Proof reading and editing will always be of great importance to writers. Students will now be ready to examine the deeper structures of their own and others' work, thinking about logical sequences of thought, format, framework, language features and effective syntactic structures as well as surface features such as spelling .

Teaching Emphases

Complementary activities provide opportunities for students to refine and consolidate their understandings of:

- meaning as a guide to spelling
- root words
- morphemic relationships
- compound words
- prefixes and suffixes
- visual letter patterns
- word derivations
- rules for pluralisation
- using mnemonics as a memory aid
- sound-symbol relationships
- proof reading.

Context 4: Independent Writing

Independent writing continues to provide one of the most powerful vehicles for applying, clarifying and further developing understandings and strategies essential to both reading and writing. As students write they develop more effective strategies and construct deeper understandings about the writing process. As they mature their writing will become more subject orientated and will encompass an ever-widening range of text-types.

Classrooms which encourage children to experiment and take risks and which give them freedom to express themselves through the spoken and written word provide contexts in which children achieve their potential as active and effective learners.

Teaching Suggestions

- Shared and independent reading provide a springboard for a great deal of independent writing. This may take the form of critique, argument, notes, reports, extensions of text, comparisons between texts etc.
- Creative and imaginative writing will continue to provide opportunities for the exploration of vocabulary and unusual syntactic forms
- Subject specific learning experiences will engender different text-types, vocabulary and forms of writing.
- Letters can be written for a range of purposes, demonstrating how vocabulary and mode of expression changes according to purpose and audience.

Teaching Emphases

Students apply and extend understandings and skills. They:

- take risks, try things out
- apply and refine concepts and strategies they are developing in a wide range of contexts
- further develop their understandings about words and the ways in which words can be modified to produce an effect
- use high interest and subject-specific words they have encountered in their reading
- further develop their knowledge that a sound may be represented by a range of letter patterns
- further develop their understanding that a letter pattern can represent a range of sounds
- apply syllabification strategies
- apply strategies for remembering the correct spelling of difficult words
- hypothesise, generalise and apply rules for plurals, doubling letters, extending words
- use strategies such as generating alternative spellings in order to select the right one
- think about word meanings, e.g. circle/circumference/circumvent/circuit/circumspect
- write as readers, realising the importance of editing and proof reading
- competently apply proof-reading skills.

When students are given opportunities to write and to take responsibility for their learning, they will apply and refine the understandings they are developing. They will realise that a good speller is not one who can spell everything right without thought, but one who can apply the right strategy at the right time, one who knows when to seek help and one who can recognise when action need be taken.

Context 5: Modelled and Shared Writing

At this phase the joint construction of texts provides an important context for more advanced exploration of meaning, structure and words. Writers become more aware of the ways in which their choice and use of words influences the meanings which readers extract from the text. Control over words is reinforced as vocabulary is extended and becomes more sophisticated. Knowledge of word derivations helps to build control over word choice and use.

Teaching Suggestions

The subject areas provide rich sources of text-types which can be jointly constructed, providing opportunities for extensive exploration of words. Some suggestions are:
- collating notes
- constructing flow charts
- writing reports on experiments or investigations
- writing summaries
- constructing arguments
- procedural writing
- descriptive writing
- writing explanations
- expository writing
- report writing
- journalistic writing.
- Proof reading becomes a major focus, as writers have become aware of their responsibility to readers and the needs of readers.
  - words causing concern are underlined. The concern could be regarding spelling or it could be to do with word choice or nuance of meaning.
  - the teacher demonstrates to students that reading as a proof reader is very different from reading for meaning.
- Use shared writing as an opportunity to further develop student's understanding of devices such as onomatopoeia and the use of alliteration as writers' tools.
- Acronyms can be explored in context.
- Words which have been invented fairly recently to serve specific purposes can be investigated ,e.g. motorway, user-friendly, hardware, windcheater, sweatshirts, runners, input, feedback.
- Model the use of a dictionary to include derivations, alternative spellings, parts of speech, pronunciation and abbreviations.
- Introduce and talk about words which have changed in meaning or acquired another meaning over time, e.g. cool, accord, terrific, high, hardware, gay, radical.
- Generalisations can be made over time about particular patterns which occur in various positions within a

morpheme or word, e.g. 'er' at the end of a word: mother, father, Peter, mixer; and in other positions: terror, fertile, literate, livery.
- Discuss homophones and homographs in context.
- Develop a list of silent consonants and group according to type.
- Reinforce strategies for remembering the spelling of difficult words:
  - identification of the critical feature of a word
  - comparing a word with one which has the same features
  - syllabification
  - isolating the root word, prefix and suffix
  - using knowledge of letter sequences and visual patterns
  - using the 'look, cover, write, check' process with a special focus on the critical feature of the word.

Teaching Emphases

Use the joint construction of texts to share:
- writing for different purposes and audiences, exploring language appropriate for a wide range of text-types
- word origins and the evolution of words
- the way writers manipulate words for effect
- the structures of words
- nuances of meaning
- proof-reading strategies
- advanced use of dictionaries
- the application of syllabification strategies
- the application of strategies for spelling difficult words correctly
- the generalisation and application of rules for plurals, doubling letters, extending words
- the technique of writing as readers, realising the importance of editing and fine-tuning of writing.

Context 6: Sharing and Reflecting

The process of reflecting and reporting on learning will become easier for students as they mature, but they may not spontaneously exercise their developing ability to reflect productively unless they continue to be given structured opportunities to do so.

Teaching Suggestions

- At this stage of development it may be profitable to build periods of reflection, representation and reporting into the regular structure of each learning component. The process will be more spontaneous and less self-conscious as it becomes a normal part of on-going teaching and learning. Some incidents may give rise to intense discussion and debate, others may be subsumed into the regular ebb and flow of classroom interaction. In all cases the process will clarify, consolidate and extend learning within the educational community and will provide individual students with a tool which will stand them in good stead in their subsequent lives.
- The classroom chart on which student's discoveries have been recorded may now be redundant. If it is still felt to be useful, it may be appropriate to condense and stream-line it, showing wide categories rather than detailed information (see illustration).

Teaching Emphases

Students may reflect on and discuss:
- rules they have constructed that relate to factors such as:
  - making words plural
  - adding prefixes and suffixes
  - contractions
  - silent letters
  - double consonants
  - the relationships of specific letters, e.g. '*i* before *e* except after *c*, except when it follows *e* or is pronounced *a*' or '*ck* is only used after a short vowel sound'
- types of words such as:
  - compound words
  - root words
  - homonyms and homophones
  - synonyms and antonyms
  - palindromes
  - words with multiple meanings
- word origins
- proof-reading strategies
- mnemonics
- word similarities, differences and relationships
- words with unusual or irregular spellings, for instance, aisle, quay, weird, forfeit
- their fascination of words
- the challenge of word play such as crossword puzzles.

Independent Spelling Phase

A B C D E F G H I J K L M N O P Q R S T U V W X Y Z

CONSONANTS: B C D F G H J K L M N P Q R S T V W X Y Z

VOWELS: A E I O U

CONSONANT CLUSTER: bl, cl, fl, gl, sl   dw, tw
br, cr, dr, fr, gr, pr, tr
sc, sch, scr, sk, sm, sn, sw, sp, spl, spr, st, str.

Digraphs: ch, ph, sh, th,   ,

Silent Letters: mn, gn, gh, ps, kn,

Short vowels: bat, bet, bit, bottle, but

Long Vowels:
a-e,	ay,	ai,	eigh
plate	pay	plaid	eight
e-e,	ee,	ea,	y,	ey
delete	feet	bead	funny	money
i-e,	ie,	igh,	y,	ye
bite	die	high	my	dye
o-e,	oa,	ow
bone	moan	blow
u-e,	ew,	ve	oo
flute	flew	blue	baloon

Other Sounds:
oy,	oi,	ow,	ou,	ir,	er,	ur
boy	coin	now	bout	stir	term	born

or	aw	au	oo	all	alk	augh
torn	awful	audience	door	tall	stalk	

RULES CONSTRUCTED BY THE CLASS

Plurals:
- Add an 's' to most words e.g. tables, chairs.
- If a word ends in 's', 'sh', 'ch', 'x' or 'y', add 'es' e.g. kiss, bus, flash, march, box, fizz.
- To words that end in a consonant + O add 'es' e.g. mango, tomato (some exceptions; piano, rhino).
- If words end with one 'f' change the 'f' to 'v' and add 'es', eg half, calf, roof. (some exceptions; reef)

Consonants:
- Double 'l', 'f', or 's' after a simple short vowel at the end of a word
- 'k' goes in front of 'e', keg, kettle, and 'i' kick, kipper
- 'full' and 'till' drop one 'l' when joined to another root, eg. useful, until.
- Omit the final 'e' from a root word before adding an ending that begins with a vowel. e.g. have - having.
- Keep the final 'e' from a root word before adding an ending that starts with a consonant; eg. care - carefully

SOME TRICKY PATTERNS: hideous; amateur; straight; height; behaviour; through; precious; sargeant; ambitious; cushion; language; weird.

For Parents

How can we enjoy exploring words together?

- Go to the library together and talk about the books you are choosing.
- Discuss newspaper articles, thinking about words which have been coined from other sources, jargon words which are coming into vogue and words which have been invented to suit a particular context. Be critical of word choice and use.
- Read and discuss articles in periodicals and newspapers which focus on word derivations and the evolution of meaning. Some of these appear regularly and can become a regular feature of family life.
- See who can complete a crossword, acrostic or quiz first. Discuss clues and share insights.
- Play family word games. Many on the market are equally attractive for grandparents, parents and older children.
- Discuss words you are not sure of yourself and ask for help in remembering them (how many 'M's in immeasurable?).

Nikki Cowsden

The Christmas Spirit

"Chou, Chou, Chou wake up," Chou was my dog, he was twelve years in dog years that is. I walked inside my clean, fresh house sorrowfully, slammed the door, and went to my room to cry because I knew Chou was dead. My room was messy and usually had clothes all over the place. I wrote on my red and white reminder pad that I had to make a grave for my cute dog tomorrow. Well I made Chou's grave which ended up covered with colourful flowers, and I prayed for him for about half an hour.

The days went by slowly and it was soon Christmas evening. I looked at the bright colourful Christmas tree that looked like a live one and saw something climb around from the tree it was Chou. I tried to catch him but every time I touched him he would disappear like a mouse and then come up in a different spot, no-one could capture him so we tried tricks but still we couldn't catch him. I know what we should do, "my friend July said suddenly. "What?" I asked. "give," "Don't say up," I said as I interrupted and walked snootily to my room.

The next morning Dad was taking down the Christmas tree. "Dad don't take down the tree, Please," I asked. "Why?"

"Because Chou might come out." But he didn't come. I watched the tree day in day out but Chou didn't come. So I thought and I decided to call him the spirit of Christmas.

uses less common letter patterns correctly.

I have blonde hair, brown eyes and a stubby nose. I am missing two teeth I have a little chin, short neck and bony shoulders. I am of a slim build and have a fair complexion. I am 10 years old and the baby of the family.

My favourite hobbies are models and coin collecting. When I was 8 I got a model car with a lot of details. When I got a plane I made it, after I put it on the delf it fell and broke in little pieces, I was sad but I got a different one which was better and I was super happy. In basketball my number is 11 last Saturday we played against Scarborough I scored 11 points, the scores were 30-31 we lost but the first game I played we won. I play for Balga.

My best colour is purple. My favourite foods are chops, chips and fish fingers. My best boys are my Keio, boomerang and my golf club. My pets are my two dogs, two cats, four birds, six fish.

Part IV:

Profiles of Spelling Development

To make recording easier for teachers, student profile sheets, that can be photocopied, are included in this book. They enable teachers to record the progress of individual students, and to compile a class profile.

The following records are included:
- student's profile sheets for self-assessment
- whole class profile sheets using all the indicators
- whole class profile sheets using key indicators only.

Note:

An individual student profile sheet that will record progress throughout the primary years is included as a fold-out at the beginning of this book.

Student's Profile Sheets

The student's profile sheets for each phase provide lists of skills, understandings, strategies and attitudes that both the student and teacher can look for when assessing spelling development.

Why use Student's Profile Sheets?

Students and teachers can work together to set and monitor goals in spelling, using the profile sheets. Students could also be encouraged to show their parents when entries are made on the sheet.

How to use the Student's Profile Sheets

The profile sheets can be kept in student's writing files and updated from time to time, perhaps in student/teacher conferences. Young students may need help to use the sheets but older students can be encouraged to take responsibility for their own spelling development.

When would you use the Student's Profile Sheets?

The student's profile sheets can be used at regular intervals or incidentally during writing conferences.

PHASE 1: Preliminary Spelling

Name: _____ Date: _____

Look what I can do	not yet	some-times	always
• I can point to my name.			
• I know the first letter of my name.			
• I know the first letter of my name when I see it in another word.			
• I know the names of some letters.			
• I can write a letter and say its name.			
• I know some parts of stories off by heart.			
• I know where to find my favourite part of a story.			
• I can read some signs I see in the street and in shops.			
• I like to 'write' like a grown-up on forms and pads.			
• I like to try and write letters and numbers.			
• I ask lots of questions about print.			
• I can write lots of things when I want to.			

• Here are some of the letters I can write:

_____

_____

PHASE 2: Semi-Phonetic Spelling

Name: _____ Date: _____

Look what I can do	not yet	some-times	always
• I can read my name.			
• I can write my name.			
• I can read some words.			
• I can write words using one, two or three letters.			
• I can find a long word in a book.			
• I know the alphabet letters by name.			
• I can sometimes link letters with sounds.			
• I can tell if a word rhymes with another word.			
• I like writing.			
• I am a good writer.			
• I am good at finding things out about words.			
• I can tell people things I know.			
• Here are some of the letters I can write:			

_____

_____

PHASE 3: Phonetic Spelling

Name: _____ Date: _____

Look what I can do	not yet	some-times	always
• I can sound words out.			
• I can spell a lot of words correctly without even thinking about it.			
• I can divide a word into syllables.			
• I can find letter patterns in words like ing, ee, oo, th, sh, ed.			
• I can find a word I want to spell by using charts in my classroom or my own dictionary.			
• I know that a letter can stand for more than one sound like A in apple, ape or Australia.			
• I know that the same letters may not always sound the same, like zoo, book and blood.			
• I can sort words according to the way they sound, the way they look, the letters they start or end with.			
• I can put words into alphabetical order by looking at the first letter.			
• I like writing by myself.			
• I like talking to people about my writing.			
• I like finding out about words.			
• When I finish writing I read what I have written.			
• I can underline a word if I think it is not quite right.			

PHASE 4: Transitional Spelling

Name: _____ Date: _____

Look what I can do	not yet	some-times	always
• I use words I know, to help me spell words I don't know, e.g. I can spell 'sign' and this helps me spell 'signature'.			
• I know some homophones, e.g. their/there; poor/pour.			
• I know letter patterns that can't be sounded out, e.g. …tion, …uit, …ough, …ight, …tch.			
• I know how to use some prefixes and suffixes.			
• I know about silent letters.			
• I know about compound words.			
• I have a large bank of words I can spell.			
• I can divide words into syllables.			
• I know how to make words plural, e.g. box, boxes; hoof, hooves.			
• I am beginning to understand when I should double letters, e.g. stop, stopping.			
• I'm very good at 'having a go' at spelling words.			
• I like thinking about discoveries I have made about words.			
• I always proof read my work carefully.			
• I know at least four things I can do when I don't know how to spell a word.			

PHASE 5: Independent Spelling

Name: _____ Date: _____

Look what I can do	not yet	some-times	always
• I can use and discuss spelling rules which enable me to spell unknown words.			
• I can make words plural.			
• I can add prefixes and suffixes.			
• I can use contractions.			
• I can use silent letters.			
• I can use double consonants.			
• I can understand the relationships of specific letters, e.g. 'i before e except after c'.			
• I can use compound words.			
• I can use root words.			
• I can use homonyms and homophones.			
• I can use synonyms and antonyms.			
• I can use palindromes.			
• I can use words with multiple meanings.			
• I can find, use and discuss word origins.			
• I can use and discuss proof-reading strategies.			
• I can make and use my own mnemonics.			
• I can notice and discuss word similarities, differences and relationships.			
• I can find words with unusual or irregular spellings, e.g. aisle, quay, weird, forfeit.			
• I enjoy the fascination of words and word play.			

Whole Class Profile Sheets

The class profile sheets have all indicators from the Spelling Developmental Continuum presented phase by phase so that teachers can enter information about children's progress in spelling. The sheets can be photocopied as required.

Why use Class Profile Sheets?

The class profile sheets enable teachers to develop a comprehensive class profile on which to base planning and programming decisions.

How to use the Class Profile Sheets?

- Collect samples of writing
- Observe children's spelling behaviours
- Highlight indicators observed
- Write entry date and highlighter colour used

When would you use Class Profile Sheets?

Although teachers make ongoing observations of children's progress, they may formally update information on the continuum two or three times each year (perhaps before report times).

CLASS

PRELIMINARY SPELLING INDICATORS

Student's' Names

The Writer:

- ◆ **is aware that print carries a message**
- ◆ **uses writing-like symbols to represent written language**
- ◆ **uses known letters or approximations of letters to represent written language**
- ◆ **assigns a message to own symbols**
- knows that writing and drawing are different
- knows that a word can be written down
- draws symbols that resemble letters using straight, curved and intersecting lines
- uses a combination of pictorial and letter representations
- places letters randomly on a page
- repeats some known alphabet symbols and often uses letters from own name
- writes random strings of letters
- shows beginning awareness of directionality
- recognises own name or part of it, e.g. Stephen says 'That's my name' looking at 'Stop'
- writes the first one or two letters of own name or word correctly and may finish with a random string of letters
- writes own name correctly
- names or labels own 'writing' and pictures using a variety of symbols
- reacts to environmental print
- is willing to have-a-go at representing speech in print form
- enjoys experimenting with writing-like forms
- talks about what has been 'written' or drawn
- asks questions about printed words, signs and messages
- is keen to share written language discoveries with others

Teacher's Notes:

Dates:

CLASS _____

SEMI-PHONETIC SPELLING INDICATORS

Students' Names

The Writer:

◆ **uses left to right and top to bottom orientation of print**

◆ **relies on the sounds which are most obvious to him or her. This may be the initial sound, initial and final sounds, or initial, medial and final sounds, e.g. D (down), DN (down), DON (down), KT (kitten), WT (went), BAB (baby), LRFT (elephant)**

◆ **represents a whole word with one, two or three letters. Uses mainly consonants, e.g. KGR (kangaroo), BT (bit)**

• uses an initial letter to represent most words in a sentence, e.g. s o i s g to c a s (Someone is going to climb a slide)

• uses letter names to represent sounds, syllables or words, e.g. AT (eighty)

• uses a combination of consonants with a vowel related to a letter name, e.g. GAM (game), MI (my)

• writes one or two letters for sounds, then adds random letters to complete the word, e.g. greim (grass), rdms (radio)

• begins to use some simple common letter patterns, e.g. th (the), bck (bike)

• uses a small bank of known sight words correctly

• recognises some sound-symbol relationships in context, e.g. points to 'ship' and says 'sh' or recognises first letter of name

• knows the letters of the alphabet by name

• recognises some words in context, e.g. "That says 'dog'"

• recognises rhyming words

• recognises and copies words in the environment

• leaves spaces between word-like letter clusters, e.g. I h bn sik (I have been sick)

• confuses words with objects they represent, e.g. 'Train is a long word, 'cos trains are long. Butterfly is a little word...'

• is willing to have-a-go at writing

• is confident to experiment with words

• talks about what has been drawn, written

• seeks response by questioning

• is keen to share written language discoveries with others

Teacher's Notes:

Dates:

CLASS

PHONETIC SPELLING INDICATORS

Students' Names

The Writer:

◆ chooses letters on the basis of sound without regard for conventional spelling patterns, e.g. kaj (cage), tabl (table), birgla (burglar), vampia (vampire), pepl (people), sum (some), bak (back)

◆ sounds out and represents all substantial sounds in a word e.g. ktn (kitten), wacht (watched), (another), aftrwoods (afterwards), siclon (cyclone), spidr (spider), isgrem (icecream), necst (next), peepl (people)

◆ develops particular spellings for certain sounds often using self-formulated rules, e.g. becoz (because)/woz (was), wher (were)/whas (was), dor (door)/sor (saw)/mor (more), hape (happy)/fune (funny), poot (put)/wood (would)

• substitutes incorrect letters for those with similar pronunciation, e.g. oshan (ocean), nacher (nature), wold (world), heard (herd), disobays (disobeys), consert (concert), butiful (beautiful), tuched (touched), daw (door), tresher (treasure), thort (thought)

• adds an incorrect vowel after a correct vowel or consonant, e.g. hait (hat), derum (drum), miu (my), fiene (fine), saeid (said), beofore (before), seing (sing)

• represents past tense in different ways according to the sounds heard, e.g. stopt (stopped), watcht (watched), livd (lived)

• uses the letter 'r' to represent a syllable, e.g. watr (water), mothr (mother)

• confuses short vowel sounds, e.g. pell (pill), yallow (yellow), u (a), pan (pen), lat (let)

• sometimes omits one letter of a two letter blend or digraph, e.g. fog (frog), mik (milk), leve (leave), plak (plank)

• still uses some letter name strategies e.g. awa (away), exellnt (excellent), mit (might), lrst (last), cav (cave)

• creates some words by combining known sight words and patterns e.g. apreesheeight (appreciate), jenyouwine (genuine), MaThursday (Mother's Day)

• usually spells commonly used sight words correctly, e.g. in, has, his, he, my, the, here

• uses some known patterns in words, e.g. ...ing, th..., sh..., nght (night)

continued on next page

Teacher's Notes:

Dates:

CLASS _____

PHONETIC SPELLING INDICATORS (continued)

Student's Names

The Writer:

- is beginning to use syllabification for spelling longer words, e.g. telefon (telephone), butufl (beautiful). Some syllables may be omitted

- identifies and uses knowledge of similar sounding words

- experiments with spelling words in different ways

- applies knowledge which has been gained from reading and words encountered in books, e.g. pirate, ship

- is beginning to use simple homonyms and homophones correctly, e.g. wind, read, park, their/there, one/won, for/four, too/to

- is willing to have-a-go at spelling

- sees self positively as a writer and speller

Teacher's Notes:

Dates:

CLASS

TRANSITIONAL SPELLING INDICATORS
(from sounds to structures)

Student's Names

The Writer:

◆ uses letters to represent all vowel and consonant sounds in a word, placing vowels in every syllable, e.g. holaday (holiday), gramous (grandma's), castel (castle), replyd (replied), gorrillas (gorillas)

◆ is beginning to use visual strategies, such as knowledge of common letter patterns and critical features of words, e.g. silent letters, double letters

• uses visual knowledge of common English letter sequences when attempting to spell unknown words, e.g. thousend (thousand), cort (caught), doller (dollar)

• uses vowel digraphs liberally, but may be unsure of correct usage, e.g. plaied (played), kaingarows (kangaroos), ailyen (alien)

• may have over-generalised the use of silent 'e' as an alternative for spelling long vowel sounds, e.g. mite (might), biye (buy), chare (chair), moste (most), rane (rain), growe (grow)

• syllabifies and correctly inserts a vowel before the 'r' at the end of a word, e.g. 'brother' instead of 'brothr', 'water' instead of 'watr'

• spells inflectional endings such as ...tion, ...ious, ...ight, ...ious conventionally

• includes all the correct letters but may sequence them incorrectly, e.g. yuo (you), shose (shoes), Micheal (Michael), thier (their), recieve (receive)

• is beginning to make spelling generalisations, e.g. uses some double letters correctly

• is able to proof read known bank of words

• is beginning to use knowledge of word meanings, e.g. sign/signature, medicine/medical

• usually represents all syllables when spelling a word, e.g. uncontrollabley (uncontrollably)

• is extending bank of known words that are used in writing, including some subject specific words, e.g. February, Christmas, restaurant, diameter, conservation, scientific

• is beginning to use knowledge of word parts, e.g. prefixes, suffixes, compound words

• uses more difficult homonyms and homophones correctly, e.g. sore/soar, pour/poor, board/bored

• is willing to have-a-go at spelling specialised words found in specific subject areas such as science and social studies, e.g. experiment (experiment), abatories (abattoirs), lattitude (latitude), electrisity (electricity)

• is aware of the importance of standard spelling for published work

• is willing to use a range of resources

• has an interest in words and enjoys using them

Teacher's Notes:

Dates:

CLASS

Students' Names

INDEPENDENT SPELLING INDICATORS

The Writer:

- is aware of the many patterns and rules that are characteristic of the English spelling system, e.g. common English letter patterns, relationship between meaning and spelling
- makes generalisations and is able to apply them to new situations, e.g. rules for adding suffixes, selection of appropriate letter patterns (-ion)
- accurately spells prefixes, suffixes, contractions, compound words
- uses context to distinguish homonyms and homophones
- uses silent letters and double consonants correctly
- effectively spells words with uncommon spelling patterns and words with irregular spelling, e.g. aisle, quay, liaise
- uses less common letter patterns correctly, e.g. weird, forfeit, cough, reign
- uses a multi-strategy approach to spelling (visual patterns, sound patterns, meaning)
- is able to recognise if a word doesn't look right and to think of alternative spellings
- analyses and checks work, editing writing and correcting spelling
- recognises word origins and uses this information to make meaningful associations between words
- continues to experiment when writing new words
- uses spelling references such as dictionaries, thesauruses and resource books appropriately
- uses syllabification when spelling new words
- has accumulated a large bank of known sight words and is using more sophisticated language
- shows increased interest in word similarities, differences, relationships, origins
- is willing to take risks and responsibilities and is aware of a writer's obligations to readers in the area of spelling
- has a positive attitude towards self as a speller
- has an interest in words and enjoys using them
- is willing to use a range of resources and extend knowledge of words, including derivation, evolution and application

Teacher's Notes:

Dates:

Whole Class Profile Sheets
Key Indicators Only

The whole class profile sheets key indicators only sheets show all key indicators from the first four Spelling Developmental Continuum phases on one page. The fifth phase (Independent) is shown on a separate page as all indicators in this phase are key indicators.

Why use the Key Indicator Profile Sheets?

The key indicators can be used by teachers to quickly ascertain children's stages of spelling development and get an accurate class profile. The information can be used by teachers to plan future teaching and allocate resources appropriately.

How to use the Key Indicator Profile Sheets

- Collect samples of writing
- Observe children's spelling behaviours
- Highlight indicators observed
- Write entry date and highlighter colour used

When would you use Key Indicator Profile Sheets?

Teachers may use these sheets to get a quick profile of a new class or to help when reporting to parents. Schools may decide on set times (say twice each year) for this information to be collected and analysed.

Student's Names

KEY INDICATORS

Phase 1: Preliminary Spelling

The Writer:

◆ is aware that print carries a message

◆ uses writing-like symbols to represent written language

◆ uses known letters or approximations of letters to represent written language

◆ assigns a message to own symbols

Phase 2: Semi-Phonetic Spelling

The Writer:

◆ uses left to right and top to bottom orientation of print

◆ relies on the sounds which are most obvious to him or her. This may be the initial sound, initial and final sounds, or initial, medial and final sounds, e.g. D (down), DN (down), DON (down), KT (kitten), WT (went), BAB (baby). LRFT (elephant)

◆ represents a whole word with one, two or three letters. Uses mainly consonants, e.g. KGR (kangaroo), BT (bit)

Phase 3: Phonetic Spelling:

The Writer:

◆ chooses letters on the basis of sound without regard for conventional spelling patterns, e.g. kaj (cage), tabl (table), birgla (burglar), vampia (vampire), pepl (people), sum (some), bak (back)

◆ sounds out and represents all substantial sounds in a word, e.g. ktn (kitten), wacht (watched), (another), aftrwoods (afterwards), siclon (cyclone), spidr (spider), isgrem (icecream), necst (next), peepl (people)

◆ develops particular spellings for certain sounds often using self-formulated rules, e.g. becoz (because)/woz (was), wher (were)/whas (was), dor (door)/sor (saw)/ mor (more), hape (happy)/fune (funny), poot (put)/wood (would)

Phase 4: Transitional Spelling

The Writer:

◆ uses letters to represent all vowel and consonant sounds in a word, placing vowels in every syllable, e.g. holaday (holiday), gramous (grandma's), castel (castle), replyd (replied), gorrilas (gorillas)

◆ is beginning to use visual strategies, such as knowledge of common letter patterns and critical features of words, e.g. silent letters, double letters

continued on next page

Dates:

CLASS

Students' Names

KEY INDICATORS

Phase 5: Independent Spelling:

The Writer:

◆ is aware of the many patterns and rules that are characteristic of the English spelling system, e.g. common English letter patterns, relationship between meaning and spelling

◆ makes generalisations and is able to apply them to new situations, e.g. rules for adding suffixes, selection of appropriate letter patterns (-ion)

◆ accurately spells prefixes, suffixes, contractions, compound words

◆ uses context to distinguish homonyms and homophones

◆ uses silent letters and double consonants correctly

◆ effectively spells words with uncommon spelling patterns and words with irregular spelling, e.g. aisle, quay, liaise

◆ uses less common letter patterns correctly, e.g. weird, forfeit, cough, reign

◆ uses a multi-strategy approach to spelling (visual patterns, sound patterns, meaning)

◆ is able to recognise if a word doesn't look right and to think of alternative spelling

◆ analyses and checks work, editing writing and correcting spelling

◆ recognises word origins and uses this information to make meaningful associations between words

◆ continues to experiment when writing new words

◆ uses spelling references such as dictionaries, thesauruses and resource books appropriately

◆ uses syllabification when spelling new words

◆ has accumulated a large bank of known sight words and is using more sophisticated language

◆ shows increased interest in word similarities, differences, relationships, origins

◆ is willing to take risks and responsibilities and is aware of a writer's obligations to readers in the area of spelling

◆ has a positive attitude towards self as a speller

◆ has an interest in words and enjoys using them

◆ is willing to use a range of resources and extend knowledge of words, including derivation, evolution and application

Teacher's Notes:
Dates:

Whole Class Profile Sheet Key Indicators Only

Acknowledgements

The First Steps Developmental Continua were written by the FIRST STEPS TEAM under the direction of Alison Dewsbury.

The Spelling Developmental Continuum was researched, developed and written by Diana Rees, Education Officer, First Steps Project, Ministry of Education, in collaboration with Judith Rivalland, Lecturer in Communications Education, Edith Cowan University.

We gratefully acknowledge the work of :
Jack Thomson (NSW) for his contribution to the Independent and Advanced phases of the Reading Continuum.
Beverly Broughton (QLD) for her ideas on reading development.
Caroline Barratt-Pugh for her contribution on Catering for Diversity and working with children for whom English is a second language.

The First Steps project acknowledges the invaluable contributions made by the schools and teachers listed below and by all the school principals who have supported their staff as they participated in the First Steps project:
- **Challis Early Childhood Education Centre**
- **Grovelands Early Childhood Education Centre**
- **Tuart Hill Junior Primary School**
- **Glen Forrest Primary School**

were involved in action research that focused on the use of different Continua.

The Project received a great deal of assistance from the following Primary Schools:
- **Carey Park Primary School**
- **Hollywood Primary School**
- **Medina Primary School**
- **Midvale Primary School**
- **Mingenew Primary School**
- **West Busselton Primary School**
- **Wilson Primary School**
- **Kalgoorlie Central Primary School**
- **Boulder Primary School**
- **Boulder Junior Primary School.**

The Project is also grateful to **Wagin District High School** in the Narrogin District and the schools in the Esperance District - the **Bremer Bay, Castletown, Condingup, Esperance, Fitzgerald, Gairdner, Grass Patch, Jerdacuttup, Lake King, Munglinup, Nulsen, Ongerup** and **Varley Primary Schools,** which, with **Jerramungup** and **Ravensthorpe District High Schools**, achieved so much in an associate role between 1989 and 1991. These schools provided examples of exemplary practice and documentation that enabled the Project team to refine and extend aspects of First Steps.

The Gosnells Oral Language Project was initiated by **Wirrabirra Education Support Unit** and Ashburton Drive, **Gosnells, Huntingdale, Seaforth** and **Wirrabirra Primary Schools** under the leadership of **Leanne Allen** and **Judith Smailes.** First Steps supported this project with funding, editorial and publishing assistance.

First Steps and Aboriginal Children

Warakurna, Wingellina and **Blackstone Schools** took part in the **Ngaanyatjarra Lands Project** coordinated by **Sandi Percival**. Action research was carried out in these schools, evaluating the use of the First Steps Developmental Continua and related materials with children from the Central Desert.
Fitzroy Crossing District High School, Gogo and **Wangkajungka Primary Schools** participated in a special project designed to adapt the Continua and strategies to the needs of children in Kimberley schools. **Margi Webb** and **Chris Street** worked with colleagues to accomplish this task.
The following schools also addressed the literacy learning of Aboriginal students as part of a special project: in the Narrogin District, **Narrogin Primary School** and **Pingelly** and **Wagin District High Schools**; in the **Kalgoorlie District, Menzies Primary School** and **Laverton** and **Leonora District High Schools** in the **Karratha District, Roebourne** and **Onslow Primary Schools**; in the Kimberley District, **Dawul** and **Jungdranung Primary Schools** and **Kununurra District High School**; and in the Bayswater District, **Midvale Primary School.**

First Steps and Children For Whom English is a Second Language

The **Highgate Primary School**, with its **Intensive Language Centre**, has undertaken a special project designed to ensure that First Steps meets the needs of children for whom English is a second or foreign language. **Anna Sinclair** was the coordinator of this Project. Extensive work, coordinated by **Kay Kovalevs**, has also been carried out at **Christmas Island District High School.**

Finally, special thanks must go to the children who have contributed their writing.

Bibliography

Bean W. & Bouffler C. 1986, *Spell by Writing*, Primary English Teaching Association (PETA), Rozelle, NSW.

Bolton F., Green R., Pollock J. & Scarffe B. 1987, *Bookshelf Stage 2, Teachers Resource Book*, Martin Educational/Ashton Scholastic, Cammeray, NSW

Bolton F. & Snowball D. 1985, *Springboards*, Nelson, Melbourne

Butler A. & Turnbill J. 1984, *Towards a Reading—Writing Classroom*, Primary English Teaching Association, Rozelle, NSW

Education Department of South Australia 1984, *Spelling R–7 Language Arts*, Government Printer, Adelaide

Gentry J. R. 1981, 'Learning to Spell Developmentally', *The Reading Teacher*, vol. 34, no. 4, International Reading Association, Newark, Delaware, USA

Gentry J. R. 1982, 'Spelling Genius at Work: An Analysis of Developmental Spelling in GYNS AT WRK', *The Reading Teacher*, vol. 36, no. 2, International Reading Association, Newark Delaware, USA

Gentry J. R. 1987, *Spel ... is a Four Letter Word*, Ashton Scholastic, Gosford, NSW

Goldsmith P. & Robinson R. (n.d.), Developing Word Knowledge (Pen Note 58), Primary English Teaching Association, Rozelle, NSW

Gosse J. I. & Harste J. (n.d.), 'It Didn't Frighten Me', *Bookshelf Stage 2*, Martin Educational/Ashton Scholastic, Cammeray, NSW

Henderson E. H. & Beers J. W. 1980, *Developmental and Cognitive Aspects of Learning to Spell*, International Reading Association, Newark, Delaware, USA

Jenkins R. (ed.) 1986, *Spelling is Forever*, Australian Reading Association, Carlton South, VIC

Ministry of Education WA 1988, 'Management and Resources with Early Years'.

Pollock Y. (n.d.), 'The Old Man's Mitten' *Bookshelf Stage 2*, Martin Educational/ Ashton Scholastic, Cammeray, NSW

Rivalland J. 1990, *Spelling Zoom Notes*, Ministry of Education, Perth

Rowe C. & Lomas B. 1985, *Spell for Writing*, Oxford University Press, Melbourne, VIC

Temple C., Nathan R. & Burns N. 1982, *The Beginnings of Writing*, Allyn & Bacon, Boston, Massachusetts, USA